W9-BNM-976

No Limits: How I Beat The Slots

A Narrative/Creative Non-Fiction Story

Debbie Tosun Kilday

Debbie Tosun Kilday

9/20/2015

No Limits: How I Beat The Slots
© 2012 by Debbie Tosun Kilday/Kilday Krafts USA

Cover Design and Photography by Deborah T. Kilday/Kilday Krafts
Editing by Michael L. Kilday
Book Design and Production by Daniel Uitti

The names of some of the characters, living or deceased, and locations in this book have been changed, as have certain physical characteristics and other descriptive details. Some of the events and characters are also composites of several individual events or persons.

The author acknowledges that she is the sole major character based on a single, real-life individual; other characters may be composites.

The author has tried to recreate events, locales and conversations from memories of them. In order to maintain their anonymity in some instances, the author has changed the names of individuals and places. The author may have changed some identifying characteristics and details such as physical properties, occupations and places of residence.

Anthony Curtis's Las Vegas Advisor
Question of the Day were used by permission.

Dedication

Kathy

Table of Contents

Foreword iv
1 – Short History Lesson................................1
2 – A Life Changing Event............................8
3 – New Worlds Open To Me........................19
4 – A New Set of Friends 22
5 – Not Bad for A Day's Work 28
6 – Come Back To Reality Or Not 36
7 – Instant Celebrity 43
8 – How Do I Act Like I Am Entitled?...........68
9 - The High Roller Coaster Ride 81
10 – Here Comes the Tax Man 93
11 – Vegas Baby! 99
12 – Don't Look Back,
        You Can Never Look Back...................119
13 – Other forms of Hard Work 128
14 – The Crumbling Cookie...........................132
15 – I Can See Clearly Now 145
16 – Forbidden Fruits of my Labor 158
17 – A New Chapter 166
18 – Is It Just Me?..168
19 – Kept From What I Love...........................176
20 – And in the End......................................186
21 – A Pro for Hire 189
Epilogue 195
Anthony Curtis's Las Vegas Advisor
Question of the Day......................................213
D.T.K. - My Tips on
Playing Slot Machines To Win 231
The W2G Slips From My Five Years
of Taxable Wins 239
Concert ticket stubs I kept as souvenirs.................239
A Sampling Of My Concert Photos & Events
At Casinos 240
End Notes 241

Debbie Tosun Kilday

Happiness comes in many forms: In the company of good friends, in the feeling you get when you make someone else's dream come true, or in the promise of hope renewed. It's okay to let yourself be happy because you never know how fleeting that happiness might be.

–Lucas Scott – 'One Tree Hill'.

No Limits: How I Beat The Slots

Foreword

People think that you can meditate and pray to God for money. You can't. If you want to pray for something let your prayers be for something that serves to help all. Pray for compassion and acceptance for all in the world. You can work hard toward your goals and give of yourself to others without wanting anything in return. In doing so you will gain satisfaction from knowing you cared, helped people and showed someone an act of kindness. Only then in your unselfishness will you see the path to riches beyond your wildest dreams.

I made over 1.8 million dollars in taxable wins in five years just playing slot machines. That did not include the small, non-taxable wins. If you added that and the comps I received, my winnings amounted to around 3.4 million dollars in all. It may sound like an outrageous number, but the following story describes how I amassed those winnings. It was my talent and I was very good at it.

Most people thought I didn't deserve to win because the money came from a casino. They would look upon it as ill-gotten gains because it came from gambling. My answer to them is: *the product of hard work is simply the product of hard work.* Gambling was hard work for me. I didn't view it as right or wrong. I just worked as hard as I could to win.

I sometimes relate to the first part of the song, "Shape of My Heart" by Sting. Even though the words relate to playing cards instead of slots, I still find a similarity to both. My relationship to the song is the fact that I have never played a slot machine for my own gain or the money I made. Although I always played to win, most of the time I helped others I thought were in need more than me. I found myself playing for the solace I would find just being immersed in the experience of playing.

It is indeed a sort of a moving meditation for me just as the practice of Tai Chi Chuan was years ago. The last line of the song greatly moves me. It explains how perceptions have been decided by others about you while the lyrics try to explain that isn't the shape of his heart. The way I interpret the meaning is the way people view others that either play cards or slot machines. The song stirs a multitude of emotions inside me and at times has made me cry. It is the stigma that is attached to gamblers. They are not thought of as the people they are inside. They are looked upon in a negative way and not as their true selves. Everyone should be judged by how much love, compassion and caring they give to others, nothing else. If you have those three qualities to show to the world you will be alright. I try to follow that rule in my own life.

Everyone needs money and I am no exception. The only difference between me and you is I am a winner because my desire is so strong I am not afraid of the consequences of winning. You must believe me when I tell you that there are consequences to winning that actually make it undesirable. There is no secret as to why I win. After many years of winning I have come to the conclusion there are only four reasons as to why I am a winner.

I am a winner by virtue of my strong desire to win, my absolute belief in my ability to win, my vision of seeing myself winning and my every intention of winning each and every time I enter a casino. Some say that you create your own reality. I would have to agree with that statement most of the time. There are variables in that you have no control over what others are trying to create for themselves which may involve you.

Never let the fear of losing keep you from playing the game.

If you can imagine it, you can have it. You are not limited by logic, the past, or the world around you. This all seems like great advice. The only problem is: how do you follow your heart's desire when it is unacceptable to your family, friends and society in general? You are shunned and ridiculed by the very people that are supposed to support and love you.

Some would say that this is a story about an unrealistic viewpoint on life. I say this is a story of a dreamer of possibilities. As John Lennon said, "I know I'm a dreamer but I'm not the only one".

No Limits: How I Beat The Slots

Quote From Albert Einstein

"A human being is part of the whole, called by us 'universe,' a part limited in time and space. He experiences himself, his thoughts and feelings, as something separate from the rest -- a kind of optical delusion of consciousness. This delusion is a kind of prison for us, restricting us to our personal desires and to affection for a few persons nearest to us. Our task must be to free ourselves from this prison by widening our circle of compassion to embrace all living creatures and the whole of nature in its beauty. Nobody is able to achieve this completely, but the striving for such achievement is in itself part of the liberation, and a foundation for inner security".

1 – Short History Lesson

A trip to unfamiliar territory to grant a dying person's wish ended up surprisingly as my destiny. My best friend Kathy had gone for a routine doctor's visit to try to find out why she was having bad headaches only to find that she had a cancerous tumor growing inside her brain. She was told she would die in a matter of months.

You would think that someone finding out this news would be devastated and prepared to die. Maybe some would but that was not the case with Kathy. Kathy, in her mid fifties, dark shoulder length hair, bright blue eyes and always wearing a big, beautiful smile, looked like she was getting ready for a photo shoot for the cover of Vogue. Instead of giving up or giving in, she planned out her days to live and did everything in her power to enjoy all that life had to offer.

In short she prepared a 'bucket list'. In it she put all of those things she wanted to do before she died. Where I came in was she needed help in getting those 'bucket list' items checked off. She recruited me as her helper or as some would say partner in living life to the fullest which to some would be construed as a crime. While my husband Mike and Kathy's husband Ned were at work during the day, Kathy was taking me off to my new day job: having fun, seeing things, trying things, not afraid of life or death. Kathy's advice to me was, "Don't be guilty about having fun or enjoying yourself. Instead be grateful you are capable of it."

Instead of staying home and being safe from harm just in case you were going to drop dead that day, Kathy and I took day trips to Madison, Connecticut to Meig's Point at Hammonassett State Park. We took in the smells of the ocean breeze, listened to the sounds of crashing waves and shore birds screaming while fighting over a piece of bread. We sat in the sun wearing no sunscreen and no concern over which SPF we should apply to our skin. We climbed up on the rocks and sat with our legs dangling over the edge as waves crashed against the rocks and soaked us. We talked about things that were on our minds, conveyed our deepest secrets to each other, and shared our hopes for the future.

At first I tried not to act surprised when Kathy told me of her hopes for the future. First and foremost, she hoped she and husband Ned would share many more years together. It was the second marriage for both of them, and the love they shared for each other made others jealous of the happiness they had found sharing a life together. Secondly, she desired to live long enough to see her grandchildren grow up and she wanted so much to be able to be a part of their lives. Thirdly, she expressed concern for her eldest daughter who was trapped in a loveless marriage. Her most earnest desire was that someday her daughter would find true love like what she and Ned shared. As she related her hopes for the future, tears welled in her eyes because the realization must have struck her that whatever time she had left wasn't enough.

I thought to myself: *How can she look forward to the future when she doesn't have any?* Then I realized I was wrong to think that way. Everyone had a future no matter how you defined it. Even if it were to be two minutes from now it was still your future. I also realized that no one should have the right to take away whatever your hopes or dreams were for the future. I certainly would not want to do that to anyone never mind have anyone do it to me.

After spending the day at the beach we ventured over to Lenny & Joe's Fish Tale Restaurant. We both decided to have fish and chips. Yes, Kathie had been given her death sentence by her doctors, but I too had lived for years with a disability. I had struggled to make believe I was fine when in fact every day was a struggle for me. Living with Chronic Lyme Disease was like any other disease. Some diseases killed you off fast while some were slow and took their time. What you chose to do in between was what counted.

I had been out of work for a long time because of my own disability and because of that I had lost touch with all of the people I used to see at work on a daily basis. Not many people realized that when you experienced a traumatic event; such as having an illness, it changed a person. When you were witnessing someone you love break down physically before your eyes until they were no longer recognizable, a little bit of you suffered and died also.

Years earlier my husband Mike and I had lost his 16 year old son Jon from his previous marriage to a car accident. Jon was a passenger in someone else's car and was not wearing his seat belt. Some would think that a quick instant death would make you think differently about the loss. True, Jon didn't suffer or even realize what was happening because it was a quick death, but those of us left behind were saddened that Jon would never have the chance to grow and experience adulthood. His loss stayed with us today and every day that we lived on without him. It didn't change the finality of it. If it wasn't for our son Kyle, we wouldn't have survived the loss of Jon. We thanked God everyday for Kyle.

In my opinion a loss is just that, a loss. Losses come in many different forms. Several types of losses are the loss of parents and loved ones through death, loss of a marriage through divorce, loss of your children leaving home and making their own way in the world, loss of the way you made your living from losing your job, loss of your ability to contribute something of yourself because of a disability. The worst kind of loss is when you have lost love in your life. The deep physical and emotional connection with another human being taken away from you can sometimes be too much to bear. Not having someone to love and nurture you and you them can make you feel like life itself has ended. A loss is something you try to get over because society told you to. You instead want to hold onto the loss as a reminder of your loss so as not to forget who you lost or what you lost.

Having grown up in the fifties I was not sure if it was a handed down principle given to my parents by their parents or if there were a group of individuals that decided one day that all persons should be happy sometimes but not all the time. My mother used to caution me by saying things to me like, "It is okay to be happy some of the time but not all of the time." She

4

would go on to tell me, "It isn't 'normal' to be happy all of the time."

I would wonder why you could not strive to be happy as much as life would allow. Sorrow had a way of showing up and butting into your fun of living. *Why not try to strive to be happy and when the sorrow butts into that happiness?* It will regardless. *Why prepare for unhappiness? Why not just be allowed to live and do the best you could while you could?*

During the last few months of Kathy's life she thanked me for taking her on our daily trips and told me that before her health started to deteriorate any further, she would like to have me and my husband Mike join her and her husband Ned to go see a comedy show at one of her favorite places, Mohegan Sun Casino in Uncasville, Connecticut. I had known Kathy for twenty five years but for some reason she had never told me about her trips to the casino. Kathy told me to not live in fear of what tomorrow might bring but instead to concentrate on this moment in time. From that day forward I took Kathy's advice and decided that I would no longer be afraid.

Kathy loved to go to Mohegan Sun Casino and had frequented there often. I had no knowledge of casinos having never been to a casino until I was close to fifty years old. I had never even thought about going to a casino. Maybe it was all the conditioning from my parents about the dangers of gambling. I found it odd that gambling was always talked about in a negative way until I started to read about the history of gambling in the United States.

Ever since the 1600's gambling had a stigma of evil doing attached to it. People usually looked at gambling

5

as a deviant behavior with no long term benefits. Yet other people sought out gambling to find a way to extend their money before they went through the mundane task of losing it to the task of paying bills. Gamblers had been portrayed by the media as low life criminal types. Generally it was assumed that they either were in organized crime or were lost souls. It would be thought that a gambler was someone that cared for no one but themselves.

A person that lost their house to a casino or took the money that would have been used to buy milk or bread for their family and gambled it away were the stories you most heard. I did not believe those things never happened. It was just as commonplace at a casino as it was at the stock market. What did you think your broker was doing when you gave him free reign with your life savings? The only difference was the broker was doing the gambling. I felt I was very capable of multiplying or subtracting from my own hard earned money myself. I also did not charge myself a broker's fee.

I came across an article recently in the newspaper about a man that was considered to be a highly respected member of the community. In the article there was a short description of him. It stated that he was a decent man, not a gambler and therefore not a degenerate. I wondered why society put labels on people no matter what they did or who they were. I also wondered who decided what people were worthy in the eyes of society?

On the night of the comedy show, my husband Mike and I went over to pick up Kathy and her husband Ned at their house. We rang the doorbell and Ned yelled for us to let ourselves in. I knew something was wrong before walking in. Kathy was laying on the couch with a blanket on her.

"I had a seizure an hour ago, but I'm ok now", she explained.

Ned was visibly shaken by what had happened earlier. He was sitting next to Kathy cradling her head in his arms. His body rocked gently back and forth as if it helped to soothe Kathy's fragile condition.

"We can't go to the comedy show with you", Kathy said with a touch of sadness in her voice.

Ned didn't say a word; just continued to rock gently. He had a look in his eyes, a mixture of sorrow and terror. He was holding onto Kathy for dear life.

"I don't think Mike and I should go either", I replied.

"You need to go places and do things while you can", Kathy reminded. Her warm smile reassured me that she was okay with not going or not being able to go. As we turned to go, I peered over my shoulder. Ned and Kathy remained on the couch as a portrait of star-crossed lovers. Ned held Kathy's hands in his as he stoked them gently. Quietly we whispered "goodnight", and closed the door softly behind us.

Debbie Tosun Kilday

2 – A Life Changing Event

My first visit to the Mohegan Sun Casino had me feeling lonely for Kathy's company. It was tough going to a comedy show when there was nothing funny about what was going on with Kathy's health.

The drive to the casino seemed to take forever. In the back of my mind I was thinking that I should just turn around and head back home. But I didn't want to hear Kathy the next day asking me all the details of the night before and me not being able to provide any.

We finally reached the exit for Mohegan Sun Boulevard. While driving around the bend towards the casino we first saw the hotel towering alongside the Thames River. It was quite the sight to behold. I had been told that the hotel design was supposed to remind you of quartz crystals towering upwards into the sky. I think that was a fitting description. We drove into an underground parking garage called Riverview and parked the car.

We proceeded toward the Casino of the Sky entrance. As we walked into the building I could feel the excitement starting to build. Inside there are an array of different textures and colors with beautiful artwork depicting Indian culture. At first you would think you were walking into a museum instead of a casino. Soon I heard the sound of slot machines playing their different tunes. The sound of coins dropping from the machines

8

into the trays below was almost deafening. People were talking and laughing as they pulled the arm of the one-armed bandits. That was the term I had heard was used to describe a slot machine taking in people's money and not giving them anything in return.

We walked to the entrance of the Cabaret Theater, gave our tickets to the attendant and we were guided to our seats. The seats were plush red velvet which seemed typical for a casino from what I had heard. A waitress came around asking us if we wanted something to drink. Mike ordered a Pina Colata with alcohol, I ordered one without. There were three comedians performing that night. Thinking back now I can't remember who they were. What I do remember was the use of swear words seemed excessive to me. My thoughts were on Kathy and the seizure she had earlier so I wasn't really enjoying the show. I don't think I laughed at any of the jokes. Even though I was with my husband and a whole casino full of people I still felt lonely – alone with my thoughts.

After the show was over Mike and I headed out to explore the casino. I needed to make some friends and to enjoy life as Kathy had suggested I do. I walked down several aisles of slot machines and looked closely at the machines trying to get a feel as to which one I might play. Nothing was coming to me so instead I started to look at the people playing the machines. Finally I came upon a row of $1 denomination machines where everyone was playing every single machine in the row and there were even people waiting in line for an opening to play. I found this to be an odd sight. It was not that they were even the same types of machines. They weren't. Yet they seemed to be in demand.

Debbie Tosun Kilday

One was a Bally's brand three coin 2x, 10x, 5x bonus times with a jackpot of up to $10,000. Another was a two coin 7x Blazing machine with a jackpot up to $10,000. There was also a three coin version of that same machine with a jackpot of up to $20,000. Another machine called "Wild Thing" had a bonus feature. If you landed on two wild thing symbols the third reel would spin again as an added bonus so that you had more than one chance to win on one spin. That machine had a top jackpot of $30,000. That seemed to make sense since it had a 12x multiplier feature.

Little did I know at that moment that all of the people playing in that row would become intertwined in my life in ways I could never have imagined. It was strange how I was drawn to a place without realizing why at the time. As time passed I figured out that everything really did happen for a reason. The people in that row all seemed to know each other and while playing their respective machines they were also having very personal conversations with their neighbors about their children, family situations and even death, taxes, politics and religion. From a distance I caught bits and pieces of the conversations. What intrigued me was the people engaged in conversation knew each other well enough to have these types of talks.

At the time I thought this must be a row of only winning machines but that was not the case. I found an opening at a dollar Bally's 2x 10x 5x machine. On my left was a man that looked like Rod Stewart's twin brother. His manner of dress at first glance was very stylish and smart yet unique. The thing I first noticed about him was his shoes. They looked very expensive. I knew they must be made of fine Italian leather made by

10

some designer. He fit the prototype of Rod the Mod, a nickname Rod Stewart had in his early days as an entertainer. I had to look at him two or three times to determine that in fact he was not Rod Stewart.

He introduced himself to me. "Hi I'm Mitch. I own my own car dealership just outside of Boston, Massachusetts. My wife doesn't gamble but she uses the points I make from gambling to buy those very expensive Swarovski crystals in that store they have in the shopping mall here. Right now my wife is getting a massage at the Elemis Spa then having her hair done plus a facial. We go to the concerts here with my points I make playing the machines. Are you new here? I never saw you before."

I thought to myself, *Gee he doesn't waste any time.* On my right was a very petite woman with short dark brown hair. She looked like a very nervous type and rigorously kept pounding the machine while puffing on a cigarette. As soon as one cigarette was smoked she would light up another. I couldn't help noticing her right leg bouncing up and down as if she was a commercial for restless leg syndrome. She wore a plain white tee shirt, black cropped pants, white cotton socks and white Keds sneakers.

She noticed me and said," Hi I'm Mindy. I told my husband I was going to the store to get a few groceries which was true only I conveniently forgot to tell him I was also coming here."

Mindy turned toward Mitch and said, "Don't bullshit".

Then she turned her attention to me. "Hey, what is your name?"

Debbie Tosun Kilday

"Debbie", I replied. "My husband Mike is somewhere playing quarter machines."

I had already played most of my hundred dollar bill into the machine when all of a sudden someone on the other end of the row hit a jackpot. The tune, "We're in the money", was blaring.

Everyone in the row seemed to stop playing their respective machines and asked all at once. "What did Nellie hit?" Mindy got up, left her machine and raced over to see.

Nellie exclaimed, "Oh my God, I hit the big one, $10,000."

Before I could say or think anything my machine started playing the same tune. It was a tune I would become very familiar with in the future.

Mindy yelled across the row. "Hey, Debbie just hit the $10,000 jackpot too."

At first I was shocked but then I looked and there it was: a 10 X, 10 X, and a red 7 which meant 100 x 100. I would be lying if I were to say I was not in shock. I had never earned or seen that amount of money at one time in my entire life. Now I was seeing it after just hitting a slot machine button. The casino immediately sent one of their VIP hosts over to me to congratulate me. He offered me a hotel room and tickets to see Paul Anka the next evening. This was new to me but I liked it. I liked it a lot. Allow me to correct myself. I loved every minute of it. My heart was pounding. The adrenaline rush was making me feel more alive than I had in years. The woman Nellie at the other end of the row was beaming also.

I thought to myself as they were preparing my money before delivering it; *What is my husband Mike going to say? Where is he?*

All of a sudden Mike came around the corner on my left and looked at me and said, "You won a jackpot? What did you win?"

I could hardly breathe but brought the words to my lips, "I just won $10,000."

Mike said, "What? 10,000 dollars? Wow."

I said, "I know, but even more unbelievable is that woman sitting at the other end of this row hit $10,000 a second before I did."

Now Mike was in shock too. Soon a parade of casino personnel came marching towards Nellie at the other end of the row. I watched in amazement as they handed her two bundles of money, each bundle containing $5,000. She smiled at them, took out a hundred dollar bill and tipped the person handing her the money. Then they headed my way.

The man holding the money in his hand said to me, "Would you like a picture taken being this is your first big win?"

I said, "Sure."

From his headset he called someone at another location in the casino telling them to come to the Sky area to take a photo of a first time big jackpot winner. Not only did they take my picture but they had made out a great big check with my name and $10,000 written on it. I still have the check and the photo of me holding the check. I will never forget the date it first started to happen to me, July 16th.[i]

I took the two bundles of $5,000 each and stuffed them into my purse. I gave the attendant two twenty dollar bills as a tip. *Now what do I do?* I thought to myself. The whole experience was still sinking in.

I said to Mike, "I think we should go home now. I don't want to walk around with $10,000 in my purse."

In unison, Cindy and Mitch chimed in. "Hey we just met you. Are you going to abandon us now?"

Nellie was at the other end of the row and even though she had just won $10,000 she was still sitting there continuing to play the same machine. I walked over to her to congratulate her on her win, and introduced myself.

"Hi, I'm Debbie".

She smiled and said, "I never have seen you here before. Is this your first time?"

"Not exactly my first time at a casino but this is my first time here and my first time playing a slot machine." I had been to Foxwoods Casino years earlier to see a show. I could never have imagined I would play a slot machine for the first time and win an amount like this.

Nellie responded, "Well it won't be your last time here after winning like that, that's for sure."

I seemed to have an instant connection with Nellie. I couldn't figure it out as to why exactly. I liked her because she was so down to earth and friendly. I told Nellie that we would be back the next night to see Paul Anka and stay overnight. Nellie told me she would be there also and looked forward to seeing me again. Before I left to go home I introduced Nellie to my husband Mike. Mindy and Mitch waved goodbye as we left.

All the way home it seemed like maybe it was a dream but I knew it wasn't. The hour and a half drive home seemed like an eternity. At first Mike and I were not saying a thing to each other except every ten minutes one of us would blurt out, "I can't believe it." and the other one of us would say: "I know". That was how most of the drive home was.

Once home I took the money out of my purse and both Mike and I looked at it. I think we both said it at the same time.

"Shit! That is a lot of money." [ii]

I took a photo of my first big win to ensure it wasn't a dream. That night I tossed and turned in my bed. I couldn't really sleep. I was too excited thinking about the events earlier in the evening. The next night we would be going back to Mohegan Sun for dinner at the exclusive and most expensive restaurant the casino had at the time. The name of the restaurant was, 'Rain'. After dinner we would have front row seats to see Paul Anka in concert in the Cabaret Theatre all compliments of the Mohegan Sun Casino.

The next night Mike and I packed an overnight bag before leaving home for our overnight stay at the casino. We both got dressed up knowing it was a special occasion. While driving on our way to the casino Mike and I were still in disbelief as to what had happened to me the night before. We both were quietly anticipating the night that lay ahead for us. This time upon arriving, I parked in the valet parking. As we stepped out of the car the attendant asked my name as I gave him my car keys. Mike tipped him with a five dollar bill.

Entering the casino we walked past several rows of slot machines as well as a section of Blackjack tables. The casino was packed with people. It was amazing to me that so many people were in one building at the same time. We finally found the restaurant 'Rain', which was on the far right end of the Sky Casino.

Debbie Tosun Kilday

Entering 'Rain' a woman greeted us at the door, asked us what our names were and led us inside the restaurant. Once inside, a man took us from the entrance to seat us at our table. We found ourselves being waited on and feeling very pampered. 'Rain' was so named because it had a wall where beads of water cascaded down. The wall was so beautiful to look at and the peaceful sound of the water made for a very tranquil atmosphere.

The five course dinner at Rain could only be described as exquisite. Each course was paired with a glass of several types of California wines to go along with the different foods. To begin the chef brought out several appetizers that smelled and looked amazing. Crab meat stuffed mushrooms, tuna tartar, bruschetta with goat cheese. Second came out a salad that consisted of romaine lettuce, arugula, field greens and strips of carrot, peppers, along with calamata olives. Third came orecchiette, little hat shaped pasta with a simple yet flavorful marinara sauce with fresh grated pecorino romano cheese topped with fresh basil. Fourth came out an aged to perfection Angus beef filet mignon with a balsamic glaze accompanied with an array of wild mushrooms. Fifth and last came out dessert which was a "molten lava cake". It was a decadent chocolate cake with a warm molten dark chocolate center sprinkled with a thin coating of powdered sugar on top. The atmosphere, staff, and the artfully prepared food made the whole experience unforgettable and amazing.

After leaving 'Rain' we headed to the Cabaret Theater. Once inside a big set of doors, I went to a podium where a very pleasant woman wearing a big smile was standing with a list of names in her hand.

16

After hearing my name and marking it off her list, she told us to follow her as she escorted Mike and I to a table right next to the stage. The theater was very beautifully decorated as are the other areas of the casino. Every attention to detail concerning the décor for it to be a breathtaking visual experience has been artfully thought out and executed. No matter what direction you looked there was art of some kind. The columns as well as the ceiling were works of art. As an artist myself I was taking all the sights as well as the sounds in.

My heart was pounding with excitement to the beat of the music. Then the lights dimmed and a spotlight shown on the right hand corner of the room. Everyone's eyes focused on that corner. All of a sudden someone brushed past my arm in the dark. It was Paul Anka. He was having fun with us by entering from the left hand corner of the room. I thought I would faint after he brushed my arm. All of a sudden the spotlight turned towards Paul Anka and us and he began to sing. As I watched in amazement, Paul Anka walked up to me, took my hand, kissed it and asked me to dance. The audience started yelling and applauding wildly, then clapping to the music as I was in the spotlight dancing with Paul Anka. I never had anything like this happen to me before. After a few twirls Paul Anka returned me to my seat. Paul Anka was a fabulous entertainer and a regular guy. He was my kind of entertainer. There was no ban on taking pictures when he performed. He encouraged it wholeheartedly.

Often he would grab the camera, place it in front of his face, strike a pose, and snap the picture himself. He would then hand the camera back nonchalantly.

Sometimes if it was a female fan requesting the photo, which it most often was, he would put his arm around the woman, drawing her close, and snap the picture of the two of them. I believe this man truly understood what a keepsake was to his fans. The flair and panache with which he did it made the men chuckle and the women swoon.

I took a few pictures of Paul Anka. He was such a first class act the first time I saw him in concert and in the subsequent times as well. Many entertainers could take a lesson from him on how to play to their audience.

3 – New Worlds Open To Me

I was feeling like I had been inducted into a royal family of sorts. I had never been made to feel so important before in my whole life. It felt good being treated so special. I was not used to this kind of treatment but after the first time experiencing it, I wanted to hold onto the feeling.

After the show we walked over to the entrance of the shopping mall and went upstairs on an escalator to the hotel lobby to check into the hotel. After getting our hotel keys we got into an elevator to go upstairs to our room. Upon entering our complementary room I walked over to look out of the window. The view from our room overlooked the river and the surrounding woods. The view was breathtaking.

I turned to Mike and said, "I just can't believe what has happened to us. It seems like we are living a dream."

As we both got ready for bed, Mike flipped through the selection of movies available to watch. They had a wide array of movies including an adult movie section.

"Maybe they have 'Debbie does the casino'." Mike said as he flipped through the selections. He glanced over at me to see if I appreciated his attempt at humor.

"I don't think we need it to get in the mood." I murmured seductively. I could see from the look in his eyes, he needed no further encouragement.

We decided to skip watching television. The intensity of the whole night's experience had excited our senses. Mike looked at me differently this night. At the beginning of our relationship long ago, he used to look at me in this way. It had been years since he had shown any real interest in me. We made passionate love to each other as if we were characters in a movie. In the back of my mind I wondered if it was the fact that I won money that excited Mike, or the money itself. It had been a long time since I had seen Mike this passionate. I decided I would just enjoy the experience instead of trying to pick it apart.

That night we slept in our complementary room in a king-sized bed with plush pillows and a soft and cozy comforter. We slept very soundly in our posh surroundings. At that moment I knew my life was changing for the better and things would be different from this point on. Not only had I made more money than I had ever seen at one time in my entire life, I was meeting new people. People that were just like me; wanting to have a conversation, eat a fancy dinner and not feel lonely. I was seeing life from a new perspective. For the first time in a long time I was feeling happy and alive. I was smiling and laughing.

After experiencing this windfall I realized how lonely an existence I had led up to this point. I felt guilty of the pleasure I was feeling but wondered why. I had done nothing illegal and I certainly was not flaunting my winnings. In fact I wanted to hide away as my mother's words danced inside my head, "You can be happy some of the time but not all of the time." It was funny how one's upbringing affected you throughout your entire life. But there was a point in time when you must break free from all that and tell yourself that you didn't have to live by the old rules anymore. I was always a rebel in the eyes of my parents. I would listen to what they had to say but that didn't mean I would do what they said. I always had my own ideas and this time would not be an exception. Debbie was going to be Debbie, not what someone else wanted Debbie to be.

4 – A New Set of Friends

As our new day started, I was still floating on cloud nine as Mike and I took the elevator downstairs from our hotel room to go eat our complimentary breakfast at Fidelia's Restaurant. The hostess at the entrance to the restaurant was cordial and very accommodating. She seated us in a booth and told us we could go help ourselves to the breakfast buffet. All the food was so artfully displayed and prepared. The ingredients used in the dishes appeared to be of the highest quality available. The orange juice was freshly squeezed and served in a cut crystal glass. After breakfast I told Mike that I wanted to go back to the same area where I had won my first $10,000. We took the escalator downstairs to the casino level.

As we approached the area known as the Casino of the Sky I saw some of the same people I had seen two nights before. Mitch was playing a 5X machine and Mindy was sitting two machines away playing a double blazing sevens machine. On the other side of the row was Nellie playing the same 2x, 10x, 5x slot machine where she had won $10,000 seconds before I had.

I said hi to everyone and they all said in unison, "Hi Debbie and Mike."

I was surprised they had remembered our names. Mindy was wearing the same outfit as the first time I had met her only in different colors. This time it was a white tee shirt, red cropped pants with white cotton socks and blue Keds sneakers. I thought to myself, *Red, white and blue, nice.*

Mindy said, "My husband thinks I am at the store shopping which is not a lie. I was at the store earlier. He just doesn't know I came here afterward."

Mitch rolled his eyes at Mindy and said, "Geez, where have I heard that story before?" Others in the row started laughing.

Mindy lit up another cigarette as she kept playing her slot machine, this time pushing the buttons instead of pulling the handle. All the while her right leg kept bouncing up and down like it was motorized. Mitch was looking very handsome with his freshly gelled blonde hair and wearing a brown leather jacket that came down to his waist. His cologne smelled nice too. I had to do a double take once again just to make sure he was not indeed the singer Rod Stewart. Mike said he wanted to go play quarter machines so I told him to go ahead and meet me in about an hour at this area.

Mike went off to do his own thing. I sat down a few machines away from Nellie and took out a hundred dollar bill. I started to play another 2x, 10x, 5x machine that was situated in the middle of the row. At three dollars a spin I was hoping I could win something again. I played the first hundred in and reluctantly took out another hundred dollar bill thinking to myself that the odds of me ever winning anything again were next to none.

As I was playing the second hundred in Nellie started to talk to me. "I come here almost every day. I only live about twenty minutes away from the casino."

"We live about an hour and a half away." I responded adding, "do you work?"

She eyed me cautiously. "Yes, of course I do. I'm a CPA in business for myself. I have three employees."

Being I was seeing her again at the casino and she said she worked, I figured she might not be that busy now that tax season was over. "I used to work for a living as a computer operator, but now I'm on disability for over ten years with Chronic Lyme Disease."

A look of concern came over her face as she asked, "How did you get that?"

I responded with, "I don't really know how it happened. At first I started feeling like I had the flu all the time. Later it progressed into muscle and nerve pain. By the time it was diagnosed, it was too late to treat it."

"That must really be terrible," she responded.

It really *is*, I thought to myself, but there was little I could do about it. Because the tick bite wasn't treated in time with antibiotics, I was left with permanent nerve damage. I had to resign myself to the fact I had the damage the disease had caused and just go on. I always thought that's what you had to do anyway – live with it.

Nellie was in her early 40's with shoulder length strawberry blonde hair and strikingly pretty. She was of medium height and on the slim side. She was dressed in layers of black on black as she had been two nights before. Looking at her she reminded me of the rock singer Stevie Nicks with her flowing multiple layers of lacy clothing.

Nellie began opening up to me, telling me how she was alone and had lost her husband to a long battle of colon cancer. They had been together since high school and had one son. Tears welled in her eyes as she told me of her husband's terminal illness and the fact that he had died so young. She had taken time off from work while caring for him at home until the day he died.

I tried to console her by saying, "I'm sorry for your loss". Then I began telling her how Mike had lost his son Jon in a car accident.

When I was finished telling her about Jon, Nellie replied, "So you understand how I feel then?"

I said, "Yes, unfortunately I do." We both shared a common bond of a painful experience others couldn't really understand unless they had gone through it themselves.

Our conversation was cut short as Nellie's machine hit a jackpot. I had not even been paying attention as I was engrossed with Nellie's life story. Her openness actually surprised me. I wasn't used to it.

Generally people liked to conceal their pain so others wouldn't see it. It was as if they were ashamed to even feel it; like sympathy was an indulgence they weren't permitted to have. I didn't mind. I liked to get things out in the open. If you did, you knew where people stood. You didn't have to guess at it. To know that made life easier. Hiding your pain just complicated life for everyone involved. I always thought: *if you can't be honest about who you are and what you feel, you can't be honest about anything else.*

Mitch yelled from the other side of the row, "Hey Nellie you lucky shit."

Nellie yelled back, "Yeah Rod Baby."

Nellie had just won $5,000 with a red seven and a 5x symbol and a 10x symbol. I thought to myself, *That is incredible.* Then I realized I had said it out loud.

I took another hundred out of my purse and after just two spins my machine hit a jackpot. I had just won $2,500. A red seven and two 5x symbols were lined up on the pay line. Again here I was, winning more money than I had ever seen at one time in my entire life. Ten minutes later my machine hit again but this time it was two 10x symbols with three bars, $3,000.

Each time Mindy and Mitch kept yelling over from the other side, "What are you doing over there? Leave some for us. Don't drain the damn machines."

Nellie and I laughed heartily at Mindy and Mitch's remarks. The day went on with Nellie winning a jackpot and me winning one right after her. Mike had come back as one of the attendants had just finished filling up my machine because it had run out of coins. I told him what had happened. He shook his head in disbelief. He started talking and playing in the same area only on the other side next to Mitch. He and Mitch found they had a lot in common and I could overhear the two of them talking sports. Both Mike and Mitch were diehard Boston Red Sox fans since birth or so it would seem. They both conveyed to each other how great it felt for the curse of the Bambino to finally be over.

I overheard Mitch say, "We don't have to listen to that crap anymore from Yankee fans".

Mike nodded his head in agreement and added, "And the best part was how they did it – by coming back from a 3-0 deficit to beat the Yankees".

Mitch smiled broadly, "That was the best part. It shut them up for awhile". They went on and on about the abuse they had suffered at the hands of the Yankee fans. I never thought much about it, but the longstanding suffering of the Red Sox seemed to parallel my own life story. Soon after they had started winning, I had started winning. Our fortunes seemed to have risen at about the same time. Perhaps it was a coincidence or maybe there was something to it.

Mindy announced. "I'm leaving... I told my husband I was going to the grocery store for a few things...that was hours ago", she added sheepishly. "My husband doesn't know I'm here so I'd better get back home." Those were her parting words. Afterward she quickly cashed out, jumped up, and dashed off. Nellie and I waved bye.

Time had passed quickly and now it was after 6pm. Both Nellie and I had learned all about each other's lives including something neither of us would guess we had in common in a million years. We shared the same birthday. I was not exactly sure how we had gotten on the subject. I think I said something about being a Pisces and how Mike was also a Pisces. That day Nellie and I realized that we both hadn't opened up and talked about what was on our minds to anyone in years, if ever. It felt good to have a friend that had something in common with me. We just talked and expressed ourselves without the fear of being judged. She listened and was interested in what I had to say. That was rare for me. I had a few friends but not anyone I could open up with and say anything to. Usually I would get a lecture from friends because I wasn't like them. People liked clones and often didn't accept you when you had a different point of view. It turned out that from that day on Nellie and I each found a true friend in each other, someone to share our thoughts with without being afraid of being ridiculed for our ideas.

5 – Not Bad for A Day's Work

During those nine hours we had sat at the slot machines I had won consistently on average every twenty minutes and so had Nellie. We both paused from playing our machines to count what money we had in our purses.

Nellie said, "I only have about $8,000 left."

I counted my money. It was not easy because my purse was of medium size and it was bulging because of all the $100 bills. I counted my $100 bills trying not to let any other people passing by see what I was doing. In nine hours time I had played some back in but had won more than I played in. Counting up my money I found I had $9,320 in my purse. *What are the odds of this happening?* I asked myself.

Mitch finally gave up in disgust and asked Mike if he wanted to go have something to eat in the VIP lounge and they could watch the ballgame in there. I told Mike to go ahead but I had already decided I was not leaving that machine. Neither was Nellie leaving her machine. After another two hours Mike came back alone saying that Mitch had gone to meet his wife back up in their room. Mike asked me if I was ready to go home because he was tired. Looking up from my machine I saw people all lined up on each side of the row waiting for Nellie or I to get up and leave our machines so that they could sit down and play them. No one else seemed to be winning at the other machines.

I said to Nellie, "Should we get up, go to the ladies room and go get something to eat?"

Nellie answered, "Sure, we need to get up from these seats. We have been sitting way too long. Let's go over to the VIP lounge."

Mike and I followed Nellie as she took us to the VIP lounge. On our way, we walked past a row of six craps tables. People were crowded along the sides of each table. We saw the roll of dice bouncing wildly off the green felt bumpers around the table. After each roll, we heard the slap of the croupier's stick on the felt as it collected the dice. The croupier then passed the dice over to the next roller. Every now and then a roar would go up from the crowd of onlookers. Craps was a very loud game that attracted a boisterous crowd. It seemed to be the noisiest part of the gaming floor by far. Cocktail waitresses hung around the craps tables eager to take drink orders. They then hurried off to fill them. Upon returning they were carrying trays full of drinks with both hands. After they carefully distributed them to the players, they took more drink orders. The cycle seemed to repeat itself endlessly.

Opposite the craps tables were banks of slot machines of assorted denominations. It was a mixture of dollar, quarter and penny machines arranged in separate rows. There was a slot machine to suit any person's tastes from the graphics it displayed to the sights and sounds it produced. All of them were designed to entice people to play. Typically there were six to eight machines in a row. At each machine sat players of all ages pushing buttons to make the wheels spin. Every once in a while a player would pull down the handle instead of pushing the button. Some people pulled the handle down really hard like they were angry at the machine. Others would give it a quick snap of the wrist. Each player seemed to have their own technique. Perhaps that technique depended upon whether they happened to be winning or losing at the time. I realized that was how the slot machine earned its nickname as 'the one-armed bandit'. It was one-armed because there was only one handle to pull, and a bandit because people were destined to lose their money most of the time.

The rows of slot machines flanked the featured attraction on that section of the floor. That was the IGT Mega Bucks slot machines. They were arranged in a circular fashion. They stood proudly on the floor, advertised by a huge neon sign above it. On the neon sign was a rolling marquee that showed the grand total to be won at any particular moment. It advanced as more money was played into the machines. The figure was constantly on the rise. I supposed it was the casino's answer to the lottery game. The odds of winning were slight, but the prize was the most money anyone could win in the casino in one sitting. These machines were 'progressive' meaning the jackpot continually grew as the machines were played. They all contributed to a huge money pot one person would take home. Normally the seats were always occupied because people knew it was going to hit eventually. No one knew when, but if you hit the progressive jackpot, you were set for life.

We crossed over a multi-colored patterned walkway that wound around the casino floor. It split and traveled in various directions like the fabled yellow brick road.

The branch we took descended down three steps onto the high roller gaming floor. 'The Pit' as it was known by people frequenting the casino on a regular basis, was the location of the high stakes slot machines and video poker games. High rollers could play machines with denominations of $5, $10, $25, or $100. I could see the higher denomination machines off in the distance on a raised floor. *Perhaps someday I will venture there*, I thought.

In the Pit money was won or lost at a faster pace because the stakes were higher. Generally only high rollers had the bankrolls in their pockets to take the risk. The numbers of jackpots won here far exceeded any won anywhere else in the casino. None but the brave, stupid or naïve were willing to take the necessary risks to win big or lose big. It could go either way. There was no way of knowing which way it would go. I guessed that's why they called it gambling.

We passed by a platform around which four $5 video poker machines were arranged in a circular fashion. It stood in front of the high roller cashier's cage and adjacent to the steps up into the VIP lounge. A few people were at the cage getting change or cashing in their chips.

I noticed the blue and white lights flashing on top of one of the video poker machines. On the video screen was displayed a royal flush, Ace, King, Queen, Jack and 10 of clubs. In the small window below the screen flashed the words -- "jackpot $20,000". Until that moment, I had never seen a jackpot that big.

We each stopped and stared in amazement as the man who had been playing the machine sat smoking a cigar with his back to the machine. He was dressed in a light blue sports jacket with matching pants, and a white shirt open at the neck with no tie. He smiled at us and we smiled back. He took a swig from the drink in his hand and put it down next to the machine.

"Nice win, congratulations". Nellie said.

"All in a day's work—been playing that machine for hours just to get my money back." He pointed at the chair next to him. "I'm going around the circle."

"Good luck, then", Nellie responded.

I poked Nellie and she turned around. "Do you know how to play video poker?"

"Not really... I tried it a few times... never won anything", she replied.

"I think I'd like to try that sometime. I'd have to learn how to play poker first though."

Nellie looked at me sideways as if to say, what for? "You'll win more at slots than video poker, besides it takes some skill to play video poker. You have to have a strategy. Slots are all luck."

I didn't exactly agree with that, but didn't say anything. It seemed to me there could be a strategy for playing slots also. Once you got the 'feel' for the machine after playing it enough times, I thought you might be able to figure out when it was going to hit. From the little I had played so far on the Bonus Times machines, I had already noticed patterns in the way the symbols were appearing. I didn't know then but I would have plenty of opportunity to test my theory later on.

Mike pointed up the steps in front of us. "Let's see how long the line is. It was pretty long earlier when Mitch and I were here."

We climbed them and peered around the corner. Several couples stood in a line that led into the VIP lounge. In the distance I saw a long cafeteria counter that had glass hoods over it. Under the hoods were steaming pans of food. Some were covered while others were not. In the middle of the counter there was a carving station. I couldn't see yet what was being carved up and served to the customers in the buffet line. Slowly the line began to shrink as people were being admitted into the seating area. I could see tables and chairs full of people eating and drinking. The whole area was a flurry of activity with waiters waiting tables and carrying drinks from the bar in the center to the tables.

When we got to the podium that stood at the entrance to the VIP lounge, Nellie took out her player's club card which had the words 'Sachem' stamped on it, and handed it to the attendant at the entrance desk. She swiped it then looked at her computer screen. After a few moments, she handed it back to Nellie and we were welcomed into the VIP lounge.

"Not everyone can get into the VIP lounge", Nellie whispered. "Only high rollers are allowed in with their guests."

As we looked around for a table to sit at, Mike said, "I'll just have some dessert and coffee. I ate earlier with Mitch. At the carving station, they are serving roast beef and turkey. It was good... might want to try that."

Mike spied a table for four over in the corner and headed directly for it before anyone else could get there. "I'll sit here and hold the table while you two get your food. Then I'll go get my dessert."

Nellie and I walked to the end of the serving line. We grabbed our plates and silverware off the serving table, and patiently waited to fill them. First I saw they had mounds of shrimp, cut up veggies, appetizers, rolls and butter, and condiments of every variety under a glass canopy on the counter. I put some cauliflower and onion salad, a few celery sticks and some radishes on my plate. Then we stood in front of two large stainless steel serving containers that opened from the top. One contained ziti and sausage. The other was a scallop dish. I passed on both and so did Nellie. At the carving table, I handed my plate to the chef. He sliced off and piled on two slices each of roast beef and turkey onto my plate. I saw a container with hot vegetable soup and ladled some into a small bowl. After we had filled our plates we returned to the table. Mike got up to get his dessert.

The dining area was on a raised platform above the Pit. From our table we could see the entire Pit. Around the back side of the gaming floor was a long row of high stakes gaming tables. The betting limit on these tables was a thousand dollars and up. The few patrons who sat at them were playing high stakes 21, baccarat, and roulette. I couldn't envision a time when I would sit at any of those tables. The stakes were too high and I really didn't know how to play those games anyway.

Mike had returned with his strawberry shortcake. As we feasted on an array of gourmet delights they were serving, we talked about our good fortunes on the slot machines. Both Nellie and I had fared very well at slots that day. Our spirits were high and our winnings were safely tucked away in our purses. I wasn't big on eating desserts but I sampled some of the strawberry slices from the strawberry shortcake Mike had gotten. The VIP lounge spared no expense on the food they were serving their high rollers. The whole experience was delightful.

Nellie and I exchanged phone numbers and e-mail addresses and called it a night after stuffing ourselves silly with all kinds of food items. We decided we would talk to each other during the next two weeks and plan on meeting two weekends from then.

6 – Come Back To Reality Or Not

During the next two weeks I planned on catching up on my life outside of the casino. There were people to see and bills to pay. The difference now was I had money to pay those bills. The first place I went to was Kathy's side. Kathy was having seizures on a regular basis now. She could not be left home alone. Her medication list was growing. The price for these medications was staggering. The medical community should be ashamed of how they took advantage of the sick and dying by writing them prescriptions for medications that didn't cure the disease. At times it eased the pain if you didn't take a look at the bill. But I noted it cost over $600 for one lousy pill. *How can that be justified?*

Kathy's husband Ned had to go to work each day so I enlisted myself to help out by keeping Kathy company. Sometimes I would go alone and sometimes I would go with my Mom. Kathy's Mom was wonderful to her daughter and faithfully joined me each day. Kathy and everyone else wanted to hear about my casino adventures. Looking back now I think I had given Kathy something to look forward to. She wasn't going to die and miss out on my stories about her favorite place, Mohegan Sun. When someone took a break from watching over her I gave Kathy an envelope filled with money and told her to not tell anyone it came from me.

"Thank you". Kathy leaned forward as best she could, as if what she had to say was for my ears only.

"You have been enlisted to win so that you can help others in need. Because of your selflessness you will continue to win. There will be no stopping you."

"You're my angel", she told me and squeezed my hand to let me know how much she appreciated me.

To this day, I wondered if she had been given some message from the other side. She fancied herself to be a spiritual person; not necessarily a churchgoer but a person who was attuned to the psychic realm. Several years before after her younger brother had died at age 40 of the same brain cancer she had, she started going to psychics regularly to try to communicate with him. Her favorite was John Edwards. He claimed to be able to communicate with those who had passed over. It seemed his specialty was easing the pain of family members who had lost someone.

In some circles he was roundly criticized for his claims, mostly by non-believers. They simply refused to believe such communication was possible. Most often these critics showed their ignorance by attacking another's belief system without trying to understand it. Because they didn't believe, it didn't necessarily mean you shouldn't. That was your choice to make. As in John Lennon's song, "Whatever gets you through the night." Who's to say what's possible?

Even though I couldn't save her, I wanted to make sure she was as comfortable and pain free as she could be. At a considerable expense, I hired a naturopathic doctor to consult with Kathy over the phone. He prescribed several natural supplements to ease the side effects of the drugs she was taking. The medical doctors' prescriptions were costing over $4,500.00 a week, while the naturopathic doctor's consultations and supplements were costing much less but showing Kathy some relief. After visiting Kathy during the day I would then leave from her house and go directly to the casino to play a few machines. After I won a few thousand dollars for her, I headed home.

After a few weeks on the natural supplements Kathy's condition started to improve. After arriving at Kathy's house one morning, I was surprised to find her up and walking again. For a change, she had a smile on her face and that was what mattered most.

"The seizures are gone for now." She announced proudly. "I just got off the phone with a travel agent... Ned and I are planning a trip to Aruba."

"What about the cancer?" I asked.

"I need to have one last vacation. I want to be able to dance one last dance with Ned." A tear trickled down her right cheek as an exclamation point. I realized I couldn't take that away from her. It sounded like a dying wish. So much had already been taken from her I didn't want to add to it. I helped Kathy as much as I could. She had special shoes made which would allow her to be able to stand and walk.

Kathy took her trip to Aruba and she did have that last dance with Ned. In the meantime I was busy at the casino winning at slots to keep up with her medical bills. Being an angel of mercy was a new experience for me. It felt good to be saving Kathy from feeling a lot of the pain her brain tumor brought on. I had the satisfaction of knowing the money I was winning was going for a good cause.

Within a few months after their return, she had been moved to hospice in the town of Branford. Even while in hospice Kathy was a fighter. The nurses there would tell her that she had to come to the realization her time was short. They advised her to prepare for death. Following their advice she just listened to soft music all day and ate fattening foods because she no longer had to worry about her weight.

Kathy's husband was very attentive to Kathy's needs and let her live even while waiting to die. One day Kathy conveyed to Ned that she was sick and tired of having to spend her last days just staying inside and listening to crappy soft music. Ned took the bed Kathy was in and started to wheel it outside into the fresh air. It was a beautiful sunny day that day. The nurses immediately rushed over and told Ned that Kathy was not allowed to go outside. He had to remind them that this was Kathy's time and all of her needs had to be met. At first they tried to stop him but they then realized he was right to try to please her.

They didn't stop him from taking her bed outside though. Kathy was so excited that she was able to breathe in fresh air instead of the sterile and stale hospital air. She was gratified to feel the warmth of the sun on her face. I remember seeing her bright beautiful smile that day. She was an inspiration for all the rest of us as to how everyone should live. Kathy passed away that year on November 3rd.

I wasn't with her on the day she died. We had seen her a few days before and she was looking weak and haggard. The cancer was taking control, and dictating its own course which wouldn't be denied. While the Morphine drip ensured she wasn't feeling any physical pain, she was emotionally distraught in her final weeks. Probably her feelings were on display during that final visit. It was apparent the end was near, and she recognized it. She was tired of fighting it. It was time to give in.

During that final visit, she said to me, "I don't want to die—I want to live." On her part, it was the final admission of mortality. She knew it had to happen. All that lived was going to die. The inevitability of death overrode your desires; no matter what they were, but you didn't have to like it. I was grateful for the times we shared together yet I immediately didn't like life as much without her in it. It was hard for me to accept losing her.

To this day I still miss her. She will be a part of me and whenever I feel like I cannot go on, I will think of her strength and try to emulate that for myself. In its own time, death will come for all of us. It can't be denied. Being a huge Star Trek fan, I recalled a line from the second movie in the series, "The Wrath of Khan", "How we deal with death is at least as important as how we deal with life." The finality of it was sobering and irreversible. You had to deal with it. Your loved one was not coming back; not at least to the same circumstance or time sequence. It was what it was.

From my first visit to the casino in July until December of the same year, I had made over $400,000 in taxable slot machine wins. That did not include the non-taxable amounts. At the end of that first year I did not have any money left except for the original ten thousand dollars that I always saved to go play again with. I had given most of the money away. I had no problem making more of it so I had no problem giving it away to others. Looking back I should have saved most of the money I won but I didn't.

In January of the next year, I got a notice from my disability providers in the mail. It notified me that because of the amount of extra income I had made the previous year at the casino they would be deducting fifty dollars from my disability check each month starting that month. I didn't think that was fair. *How could they take money away from my disability check each month just because I had gone to a casino?* I was still disabled. I wondered what one had to do with the other. *How could they be sure I would keep going or that I would continue to win?* Whatever the answers were didn't matter. They were taking fifty dollars away from me. The disability providers had made their arbitrary decision. I hadn't realized that there would be consequences to winning. I thought that was always left for the losers. I would find out later that there were consequences for both winners and losers. In fact winning was more dangerous than losing. If you were a loser you made the powers that be happy. The casino gained more money, you gained more points, got more perks, all for being a loser. People related better to you as a loser. You were one of the masses.

My circumstances were different. I kept winning much more than I played back in. The casino had to keep paying out to me. I wasn't going home with empty pockets. The only way I got any perks was to keep playing for long hours but even then I always went home with more money than I came there with. My only redeeming quality in the eyes of the casino personnel was the fact that I drew a crowd of people each and every time I was there.

Debbie Tosun Kilday

As one of the slot attendants once told me, "You are a great draw. It is good for business."

I began to feel like an attraction; as if I was one of those show ponies where all the kids wanted to sit on the pony's back to have their photo taken. It was not that the kids liked or had any concern for the pony at all. They just wanted to make sure they had proof they were at the event so they could grab some attention for themselves. It was a sign of things to come.

7 – Instant Celebrity

I got a notice in the mail about a promotion the casino was holding on January 6th. All you had to do was tear off the ticket attached to the notice which had your name and players club number on it, bring it with you and put your ticket into the barrel. If your ticket was drawn you could win one of 10 prizes totaling $50,000. The first prize was $20,000. The second Prize was $10,000. The third prize was $5,000. The fourth prize was 10 winners of $1,000 each. The fifth prize was 10 winners of $500 each.

I looked forward to going to the casino that night but earlier that day I had gotten a call from a family friend that I used to work with at a local factory for over ten years. His name was Ben. I had gotten to know Ben's whole family through the years I had worked with him. Sometimes I would drive Ben to work and bring him home if the weather was bad during the winter months. Ben was like a father figure to me. I hadn't heard from or seen Ben for several months even though we tried to keep in touch after the factory closed. Ben had asked me how I was and asked if I would meet him for lunch. I told Ben I didn't really want to go to lunch that day but would plan on meeting him at another time.

Usually I told Ben what was going on in my life since the last time we talked but this time I didn't. I deliberately kept my casino activity from him. I wasn't sure why I did that but looking back I think it was because I didn't want to be asked questions. I also did not want to talk about all the money I was winning for fear of sounding like I was bragging. No one ever told me their personal business but always wanted to know mine. Even now when I am asked all kinds of questions, others don't reciprocate. It was as if I was expected to want to share but they didn't have to.

When Mike got home from work that day, I told him about the drawing at the casino. "I'm going to win big tonight."

I didn't know why but I had a feeling that evening would be a memorable one. When I had these 'feelings', often it seemed that they came true. I couldn't explain why to anyone so I usually didn't bother to. I figured they should accept my premonitions without explanation just as I did.

"I can't go with you. I'm on call. There's a special project going on at work and I might be called to go in at any time."

It didn't appear he wanted me to go, but heard the determination in my voice, and figured it was pointless to try to talk me out of it. Once my mind was set on doing something I just did it. What others may have perceived to be a streak of stubbornness, I considered being determined. In this case, I just knew I was going to win that night at the casino. I was determined to.

Mike asked me. "Why are you so sure you are going to win?" Mike was a computer programmer. He was used to dealing with machines and their programs. For the past three decades, he had dedicated himself to fixing problems that arose. When dealing with computers, results were predictable if you understood the programming. To him, there was a logical reason for everything that happened. People, however, weren't always predictable, and they weren't always logical. There were a lot of unknowns.

"From now on," I said, "I am not going to lose. Every time I go there I will always win something."

"Why do you believe that?"

"I just know".

In resignation, he shook his head like this was a problem he didn't know how to fix. I knew he didn't understand, but I couldn't explain it any better. I just knew. When you couldn't explain your belief system to other people you came off as being a little conceited to some, or just a little 'off' to others. You just had to let that go, and stick to what your gut was telling you – believe in yourself. *At that moment my motto became what it remains today: I am a winner by virtue of my desire, belief, vision and intention.*

When I arrived at the casino, I took a quick pass through the casino. I went directly to my favorite row of machines. Nellie was home sick with a cold and had told me she would be unable to meet me there. I wasn't sure about the others so I thought I would check the area to see who was playing. None of the regulars were there playing; just several players I didn't know. I wasn't sure why but I was determined to play another type of machine, other than Bonus Times, to prove to myself that by sheer determination alone I would continue to win. First though I had to go to enter the drawing.

Entering the ballroom where the drawing was being held, I walked up to the barrel. As I slipped my ticket into the slot in the barrel I hoped I would win something. Usually when Mohegan Sun held special drawings of this kind, they went all out. The ballroom was decked out with streamers hanging from the ceiling and balloons taped to them. They waved to and fro as the crowds milled around them. Strategically around the ballroom, three long tables were set up with salads, sandwiches, and assorted finger foods for attendees to munch on. Attendees lined up along them picking through the food items, and filling their plates. Arranged around the floor were tables and chairs for patrons to sit at while they ate. A DJ was stationed at the back of the room playing contemporary music.

I took a quick look around the floor to see if there was anyone there I recognized. I couldn't spot any of the regulars I usually played slots with. Over the public address system the DJ announced that the drawing would take place at around 10:15pm. Since it was close to dinner time, I made a salad for myself and sat down at one of the tables to eat it. While I ate, I watched the crowd shuffling past and thought, *they certainly get a large crowd for these events*. When I finished eating, I didn't see much reason to remain there for the next three hours waiting for the drawing. It was only 7:30pm so I decided to go try my luck in another area of the casino and play different types of machines just to see what would happen.

I ventured over to the Casino of the Earth. It was where I didn't play much. I had brought $1,000 with me to the casino that night to play. I sat down at a Double Diamond $1 machine which was 2 coins per spin. I sat there and played hundred after hundred without winning a thing. Of the $1,000 I had brought with me all that was left was two hundred dollars. I got up and walked away from the double diamond machine and started walking through the VIP area where the higher denomination machines were. I was so disgusted with myself over losing almost a thousand dollars. Throwing all caution to the wind, I sat at a two coin $5 Triple Strike machine. Each spin was $10. In seconds one of my last remaining hundred bills was gobbled up by the machine. Still I had not won a thing. I put my last hundred into the machine. I played it and got nothing. Now I was out of money.

I was about to take my players club card out of the machine and go home when a slot attendant came up to me. He was neatly dressed in his slot attendant uniform, a white shirt, black pants and vest. "We have been looking for you. We tracked you through your player's club card to find your location."

I said, "Why, what did I do?"

He said laughing, "Nothing, but why weren't you at the drawing at 10:15 pm?"

I said to him, "Did the drawing already take place?"

He said, "Yes it did."

I looked at my watch and noticed it was now 11 pm. I had forgotten all about the drawing.

Smiling broadly the attendant announced, "You won a prize in the drawing."

"I did? What was it?"

"You won the top prize, $20,000. Come with me to the office to claim your prize."

I couldn't believe my ears but now I knew more than ever that I was a winner. I did try to keep it in perspective about what had happened earlier. I had lost a thousand dollars playing a variety of different slot machines. I felt very irresponsible and wondered if maybe I was turning into one of those degenerates people liked to talk about. I had that thought for a split second; then I remembered I had just won $20,000.

I followed the attendant to an office next to the VIP lounge in the Sky Casino. Above the door a sign read 'Credit Services'. I hadn't seen this area before, and wondered what that meant.

"What exactly does credit services mean?" I pointed at the sign above the door.

The slot attendant replied. "This is the place where players get their markers, and also pay them back."

"Oh…what's a marker?"

"The casino lends money to special players with the promise to pay it back within five days."

It seemed odd to me that people would gamble with money they had to borrow. But then I thought that wasn't too different from how a bank operated. The casino was just doing what a bank would except it was on the casino's turf. Giving players money to play with kind of made sense. The casino would get it back one way or the other; just like the bank would.

Once inside I signed a form to claim my prize. I was given four bundles each containing $5,000 in cash. Along with it I received a hearty "Congratulations" from each person in the office.

I was so excited but had no one to share this wonderful news with. I called Mike at home to tell him what had happened. Mike answered the phone but his voice sounded funny.

"When are you coming home?"

"I just won the $20,000 first prize in the drawing." No sooner had I told Mike my news, there was dead silence at the other end of the line. I thought I had lost the cell connection. I wondered why he wasn't excited over my news.

Then he continued in a low voice, "I just got off the phone with Ben's oldest son..." His pause was ominous. "Ben passed away this afternoon."

My excitement quickly turned to sorrow. I wasn't sure how to feel at that moment. I was happy about winning all that money but so sad hearing the news of my friend Ben's passing. My thoughts returned to earlier that day when Ben had called to ask me if I wanted to get together for lunch and catch up on old times. I felt horrible that I had not met him for lunch. Now I would never see him again. Many thoughts were racing through my head at that moment but the one I remember thinking was that life was so short. I didn't want to go right home now. I wanted to stay where there were lots of people to drown out the emotions I was feeling.

"I won't be coming home right away. I'm going to play a few more slot machines before heading home."

Mike seemed to understand what I was feeling without me having to explain it to him. All he said was, "Don't stay out too late," and hung up the phone.

It was already 11:45 pm. As soon as I hung up my cell phone I noticed I was very near the high roller area of the Sky Casino which regulars affectionately call 'The Pit'. The reason it was called The Pit was because you had to walk down a set of stairs in order to enter or exit the area. I figured I had a bit of money to play so I walked over to a three coin $5 machine called, 'Triple Lucky'. It would cost me $15 a spin.

So far the night had been a mixed blessing. I had won $20,000 and lost a father figure at the same time. I didn't know if I should feel happy at my good fortune or grieving for my loss: *What else might happen?* I was going to find out.

A young man was sitting next to me and he seemed to want to talk to someone. He smiled at me so I smiled back. I figured I would start the conversation.

"What's your name?"

"Mark." He replied. "I'm a graphic designer. I own my own business. I come here occasionally to unwind."

"Are you self-taught?"

He shook his head no. "I went to school to learn it".

"I have learned what I could on my own." I continued. "I take pictures and make greeting cards".

He nodded in response but his thoughts seemed far away. Mark was a young man in his mid-thirties. He had a sadness about him that was hard to fathom. With his mustache and shaggy dark black hair, he had the look of a swashbuckler. All he needed was a wide-brimmed hat and a parrot on his shoulder, and he could pass for Blackbeard the pirate. He tried to look like he didn't have a care in the world. But it was easy to see through that if you knew what to look for.

Finally I blurted out, "About an hour ago I won a huge jackpot and at that same moment I found out a dear friend of mine had passed away."

Mark seemed in the mood to share his troubles. "My girlfriend broke it off with me tonight because I come here and gamble and no one in her family will accept the fact that I come to a casino. Tonight I proposed and she turned me down. What do you think of that?"

I answered. "I think that unless you are hurting someone, it's none of anyone's business what you do."

Mark leaned to one side and took a ring box out of his right pocket, opened it and showed me a gorgeous solitaire two carat pear shaped engagement ring in a platinum setting. I know about diamonds and different types of metals. In my youth I had worked as an apprentice at a jewelry store and had learned how to cut and grade diamonds.

In a sympathetic voice, I said, "Your girlfriend broke it off with you because of what her family thought?"

With his eyes cast downward, Mark nodded his head yes. I felt sorry for him. In the past I had similar experiences with family and friends. No one felt sorry for me. When you didn't meet someone else's expectations, you were automatically to blame regardless. Even though no one was really to blame, it hadn't worked out that way for me. If you couldn't meet their expectations, you were at fault rather than them. Long ago I had given up trying to please anyone else. It was a losing proposition.

I asked, "Will you stop coming here to get her back?"

He shook his head no and then turned towards me and said, "I come here after working all day, dealing with customers and just want to unwind. I'm only here once or twice a week an hour or two tops and when I am here I win a bit of money. What's wrong with that?"

I really didn't have anything to say at that comment being I completely agreed with what he said. I decided not to say anything at all and just shrugged my shoulders. All the while I was playing the Triple Lucky machine. Suddenly the machine went off. I had won a jackpot. Two triple lucky symbols came up with a red seven. I had just won $13,500. [iii]

My new found friend Mark said, "Wow, you are lucky." Just as he uttered those words his machine called a Red Rose hit a jackpot of $4,000.

Mark looked at me in amazement. "I think the luck is coming from you, I can almost feel the energy. I want to play next to you from now on when I come here."

I laughed at that comment because I was hearing comments like this more and more while meeting people for the first time. In general gamblers were superstitious, some more than others. At the same time I had to admit to myself that I was really lucky most of the time. Once Mark and I got paid for our wins from the slot attendant I took him into the VIP Sachem Lounge. We sat on a comfortable couch that felt and looked like red velvet. We ate some food, had a few drinks and chatted, exchanged phone numbers and then called it a night.

Driving home I thought about the whole night. I started to wonder if certain types of slot machines won more consistently than others and if so, why. That night I decided I would try to be more observant of the machines while playing them. I had money now to try my luck without worrying too much about losing it all.

When I got home Mike was waiting up for me. I was about to tell him what had happened but instead I took the four bundles of money out of my purse totaling $20,000 and laid them on the comforter on our bed. Mike just stood there with his mouth open in amazement. I didn't even tell him about the other thirteen thousand five hundred because it didn't seem that important at the time. That night I took a photo of my ticket drawing win.[iv]

I was an instant celebrity. Pulling a handle on a slot machine may or may not make people think you were lucky when you won. On the other hand, your ticket being pulled out of a barrel containing over 200,000 tickets made people realize you must be lucky. I wondered what I should do with the money. This would take some thought.

I was totally unprepared for what was happening to me. I barely slept that night while thinking of the twenty thousand dollar drawing win, the thirteen thousand five hundred dollar win at the Triple Lucky machine, and my friend Ben dying. Meeting Mark who was so young and successful yet was rejected by loved ones because of his visits to the casino put it in perspective. Besides the twenty thousand plus thirteen thousand five hundred, I still had money from the two weeks before plus the original ten thousand dollars that started it all.

The next morning I told Mike that we should plan a trip to The West Coast in November to spend Thanksgiving with our son Kyle. Our only son Kyle was now living on The West Coast working in the television industry. After losing Jon and now with Kyle living 3000 miles away, perhaps both Mike and I were feeling a bit of the empty nest syndrome. We planned our trip to the West Coast and looked forward to Thanksgiving time.

In the weeks and months ahead I split my time between being home and being at the casino. I won on average up to $7,000 a night. As fast as I won money, I spent it. I gave to individuals I felt were in need. Looking back now, I realize the only ones I didn't care for were Mike and myself. The money I was winning didn't seem real. There was too much of it. Before now I never had money whereas now it seemed hundreds of thousands of one hundred dollar bills were passing through my hands.

I started playing different types of slot machines and I would experiment how I would play them to see if playing a machine a certain way would make it win more. After learning all I could by playing the different slot machines, and by comparing notes with other people who played them often, I was beginning to understand how the machines worked. Just by observation I was able to predict by looking at the face of the machines and the location of the numbers and symbols which machines were ready to hit. No one would believe I could predict which machines would be winning next just by looking at them. People would refer me to different types of books on playing slot machines where all of the experts would say that it was all random and there was no way to predict a winning slot machine. True or not I was certainly winning more than I was playing back in. I was showing a net gain.

One night Mike and I met Nellie at the casino and saw that the two slot machines where we had met were available. We decided to play the same machines to see if we could win again like we had before. Mike decided he would play the machine that was in the middle of that row. I had found that in order to have a chance of winning on a dollar machine you had to play in at least $300 most of the time to be able to see if the machine was ready to hit.

Nellie won a thousand dollars on her second spin. I won five hundred dollars a few minutes later. This night wasn't going very good for me because I was not winning big amounts. After winning thousands of dollars I was not satisfied winning five hundred dollars.

Mike had already put in three hundred dollars into his machine and had won nothing.

He got up off the machine and said "I'm going to play the Sizzling Sevens." It was his favorite quarter slot machine.

I looked over at the machine and saw that by the position of the numbers and bars that his machine was almost ready to hit big. "Don't you dare move... that machine is going to hit. Keep playing it."

He resisted. "Why are you saying that? You must be crazy. There is no way you can predict the machine is ready to hit."

I took out a hundred dollar bill out of my purse. "Put this in the machine. If it doesn't hit with that hundred dollar bill, you can go play anywhere you want."

Mike put the hundred dollar bill in and began to spin the machine. He was about halfway through the hundred dollars when—the numbers started coming down one by one; first the red seven, then the 10x symbol, and finally the last 10x symbol. Mike was sure glad that he had not left that machine to go play a quarter slot machine. A $10,000 win was not something you ever wanted to walk away from. That night I took a photo of Mike's $10,000 jackpot. [v]

The casino and the people that worked there made me feel like I belonged. Even though loneliness had seemed to bring us all together at that location we all now had people to relate to. It took my mind off of what was happening in my real life outside the walls of the casino. An empty house, sick relatives, dying loved ones, a world filled with pain, suffering and loss. Nellie would meet up with Mike and I and the three of us would spend our time together playing the slot machines sitting side by side.

Sometimes we would all go over to the Casino of The Earth section late at night to the Feather VIP lounge. It was located behind the Wolf Den where bands played on stage for all to see and hear for free. The Wolf Den was centrally located in the Earth Casino. As you walked towards the Wolf Den you could see gray animated wolf figures that overlooked the stage area near the ceiling. Every so often the wolf figures moved their heads up and let out a howl as they wagged their tails. This area was frequented mostly by oriental people that played table games like Baccarat, craps, and Gai Pao poker.

It became a habit for us to visit the Feather VIP lounge after midnight. The oriental chef would come in after midnight each night to make his specialty dishes. One of his signature dishes was freshly made Wonton Soup. The wontons were made by hand fresh each night. We would sometimes just stand near his cooking station to watch him work. Each wonton was a work of art and very tasty. After having his wonton soup you would never settle for any other version found elsewhere.

Spending time with Nellie was like spending my time with a close family member. It was like Nellie had been a lifelong childhood friend yet we hadn't known each other that long of a time. Mitch joined us on occasion when he was able to get away from his business. Mitch had his moments when he would win big too. Mitch would ask me what machines he should play. Following my instructions he did win and he won big. I would tell him to look for certain things like a red seven on the far right on the line not the first or second position would give him a clue that the machine was about to hit something big.

Slowly I was beginning to devise a formula for winning at slot machines just from observation. Mitch was the first I shared this information with. I noticed the symbols on the machine had to be in certain positions before a jackpot occurred. *It is significant when a red seven comes down on the line in the first position on the far left. It is true that something big is about to be won. But if you just see the red seven come down first and nothing else to go with it, you can be sure it would be a long while before that machine hit a jackpot. If you see the red seven in the last position on the far right, the machine is ready to hit a jackpot. The missing bit of information is just how close is it? The pattern of symbol behavior is the key.* Once I figured that out, I would know not only how to play any machine, but when to play any machine.

Mitch asked me for my e-mail address and cell phone number. He started e-mailing me asking when I would be at the casino. I would e-mail him back telling him when we would be there. Mitch started to only come to the casino when he knew I would be there. As rumor would have it, people started talking about me. My reputation for winning was getting me noticed. People started to gather around me wherever I was playing.

On one particular night after seeing Kathy Griffin the comedian in the Cabaret Theater I felt like going off by myself where I knew no one would be looking for me. I felt like losing myself in playing a slot machine and didn't want to be bothered by a crowd of people. I went off to a remote corner in the Earth Casino and started playing a random machine I had never played before. I was doing well and winning small amounts consistently. I felt relieved that I could just sit and play. No one seemed to know me in this area of the casino. It was quiet and no one else was playing there except me. I played for several hours and then someone came and sat down at the machine two seats from me.

I didn't even look up to see who it was. After awhile I felt like that person was watching me so I turned to look at them. At first it was hard to recognize her without her well groomed hair and perfectly airbrushed makeup that hid her freckles while onstage. This person was wearing no makeup and had her hair piled on top of her head secured with a few clips. She was wearing an old worn out looking pair of grey sweat pants with a beige tee on top. It was Kathy Griffin.

I looked at her and she looked at me. I could tell she was hoping I would not recognize her. She too had come to this remote corner to try and hide out from fans and just be left alone. I smiled at her and she smiled back shyly. I started the conversation.

"Are you trying to hide away like me Kathy? Don't worry. If you don't tell anyone you saw me, I won't tell anyone I saw you either."

At my remark, she cracked a smile like I read her mind. I imagined even celebrities needed some alone time. The demands on their time left them with little or no time for themselves. In recent weeks, I was beginning to feel the same way. We were both performers in our own way.

"What's your name?" Kathy asked.

I replied, "Debbie."

"Are you some sort of celebrity where you would have to hide out too?" Kathy asked as she pulled the handle on the Haywire slot machine she was playing. The wheels clicked and each real spun once to a stop in rapid succession.

I said, "Yes, sort of. I win tons of money just playing slot machines so I have a bunch of people that try to follow me around with hopes that the luck will rub off on them. Tonight I wanted to just come here and play where no one would guess I would be playing."

Kathy nodded her head in agreement."I can relate to that. Where do you usually play in case I want to come stalk you?"

"I usually can be found in the Sky Casino playing the Bally's Bonus Times machines. There's a row of them near the Brookstone store at the end of the shopping mall." I didn't know why she was asking. It could have been that she wanted to see me again or wanted to try out those machines.

After those few words we just played our respective machines the rest of that night. We showed our mutual respect for each other, just wanting a little alone time. Kathy was booked for the whole week in the Cabaret Theater so I knew I might encounter her again.

Two nights later I secured four tickets to see Kathy Griffin. Mike and I had invited a couple, Jennifer and Jake, that we liked to hang out with. We had been to quite a few concerts together and had fun each time. They weren't the type of people that demanded anything which was refreshing. Other couples we knew had certain expectations and voiced them to me. Jennifer and Jake always offered to pay their own way, but we never accepted any payment from them. It seemed enough for us that they offered to pay us anything. They appreciated the good times we shared together and we enjoyed each other's company.

Before going to the show I treated the four of us to dinner at Jasper White's Summer Shack. It was a relatively inexpensive place to eat at Mohegan Sun considering the other choices offered. Primarily they had a variety of fresh seafood on the menu. Each day they listed several specialties of the day on the blackboard on the back wall of the restaurant. The print was large enough so it could be seen from anywhere in the restaurant. That day the fresh fish selections were: local Bass and Bluefish, Mahi Mahi, Arctic Char, and Atlantic Swordfish. Like everything else at Mohegan Sun, there was always more than one choice offered.

The restaurant was on two levels. In the balcony section, there were tables with padded chairs. On the lower floor, rows of picnic tables and benches were arranged on both sides of the floor. I imagined it gave the impression you were attending a backyard barbeque. On all of the serving tables they usually put down sheets of brown craft paper. It made cleanup very quick and easy for the staff. They just picked up the dishes and rolled up the used brown paper sheet. Then put down a new sheet for the next group of diners.

Since there were no reservations taken at Summer Shack, they put you on a list and you just waited until you were seated. High Rollers often got preferential treatment so we were seated almost immediately. We were led by the hostess to a booth against the far wall under the menu signs. Summer Shack was always a good place to go eat because you always knew you would have an excellent meal and the service was quick and friendly. The atmosphere was casual there. They also had an extensive list of imported beers. Mike and Jake tried different ones at different times.

After dinner while they were sipping on glasses of German beer, I told everyone how I had met Kathy Griffin two nights before while we both hid out from fans. I could tell by the looks on the faces of Jake and Jennifer, they didn't believe my story. I just shrugged it off.

"I find that hard to believe". Jake protested. "Why would she single you out?"

"I don't know, but it's true". I said.

Then Mike chimed in. "The celebrities who perform here have been known to go out on the casino floor. Steven Tyler and Joe Perry did it a month ago when Aerosmith performed in the Arena. The night before the concert, I was told by some players that they were on the casino floor playing slot machines. One guy told me he had a conversation with Tyler. He said he acted just like a regular guy."

Jake made a face like he didn't believe that either. He downed the rest of his beer in one gulp and made a move to pull away from the table. Mike did the same, and started to reach for his wallet. I slapped my player's club card and driver's license on the bill. The waiter came by, looked at my driver's license, and rushed off with the player's club card and bill to process it.

Jake looked over at me. "You think you can get me Kathy's autograph?" The look on his face when he said it suggested this was a test.

"I'll ask her when I see her." I played along suspecting I just might see her later.

Jake smiled slyly, "Ok...it's a deal. When you see her, ask her."

"Let's go see Kathy," Mike teased. "The Show is going to start in 30 minutes. There'll be a line to get in".

"I'll pay the tip", Jake said.

"$25 is about right". Mike offered, "Thanks, Jake."

"Don't mention it. You guys have given us plenty of tickets in the past." Jake put the tip on the bill, and pointed at the waiter. He came over and picked it up.

"Thank you sir; enjoy your show."

We quickly filed out of the restaurant, made our way to the escalator, and took it down to the casino floor. When seen from above, the floor appeared to be speckled with flashing blue and white lights atop many of the slot machines. That was good news for slot players. That meant the machines were hitting tonight. Jackpots weren't necessarily predictable, but some nights were better than others. I always suspected that was due to the number of people playing. Tonight being a Saturday, a lot of people were playing. The walkways and casino floor were jammed with people.

We made our way to the line going into the Cabaret Theater. As usual we chatted with people who were in line. As we neared the entrance, the talk turned to that night's entertainment. An older couple immediately ahead of us in line was discussing their many trips to see comics at the Cabaret. A woman decked out in a red sequined dress and a string of pearls around her neck remarked, "I hope she doesn't swear a lot. It seems whenever we see a comic in the Cabaret, every other word is a swear word. I don't like that."

I reassured them. "She doesn't swear much. That's not her act at all. She does have some pretty funny things to say about celebrities. She likes to pick on celebrities. Her act is mostly celebrity gossip."

As was the custom of the Cabaret, we stood at the reception desk and waited to be escorted into the theater. The attendant took my name, and handed a card to the hostess. "Nice to see you again, Debbie. Have a fun time."

There was no assigned seating per se. The hostess escorted us into the area in front of the stage and gave us a choice of available seats. We selected four seats on the right side of the floor. A waitress passed by shortly thereafter and asked for our drink orders. Mike and Jake ordered bottles of Sam Adams, Jennifer ordered a glass of wine, and I ordered a vodka and tonic with a lemon and lime wedge.

The house lights dimmed and Kathy Griffin strolled on stage. As I had predicted, the topics for the evening were Brittney Spears and Lindsay Lohan, Kathy's favorite targets. In the spirit of good-natured fun, it was all harmless comedy, unless you were Brittney or Lindsay of course. She had the crowd roaring in a few minute's time. Kathy had a way of making the mundane seem hilarious.

One item she added to her routine was her experiences on The View. That was Barbara Walter's show on which Kathy was a guest several times. Kathy's favorite target on the show was Elizabeth Hasselback. No one really saw what was going on behind the scenes. According to Kathy, her off-screen arguments with Elizabeth were legendary. It seemed Kathy took great joy in making Elizabeth squirm.

After the show we made our way through the crowd. I wandered off to play my favorite machine, the Bally's

Bonus Times. Mike, Jake and Jennifer wanted to play near me in hopes I would bring them luck that night.

I met up with Nellie, Mitch and even Mindy was there. The whole gang was back together and we all were playing on both sides of that whole row of machines. I was winning a thousand dollars over and over again. [vi] Everyone was happy and having a good time. I was having fun so I started spreading hundred dollar bills around to everyone so that we all could continue to keep playing into the night. At around 1 am I still was playing at the same machine. Some of the others had switched to playing different machines.

All of a sudden Kathy Griffin walked into the area with her tour manager and bodyguard Tom. He was a handsome guy of average height with short dark hair in a crew cut style. This time she was wearing her celebrity face for the crowd. She was loud and wanting to be noticed.

She came over to me and gave me a big air hug and said to me, "I hope you don't mind Deb that I came to bother you again."

I replied, "No not at all, have a seat." Before my friends could close their open mouths as they stared at Kathy, I hit a jackpot on the machine again.

Kathy said, "Deb you weren't kidding when you said you win a lot. I wish I could win like you. What did you win Deb?"

I answered, "Ten, thou--sand doll—ars."

I had just hit the big jackpot once again. At that moment everyone started screaming and Kathy started jumping up and down waving her hands wildly, definitely drawing attention to both herself and to me. [vii]

After I got paid for that jackpot, Kathy quieted down and resumed playing slots on her machine. I spied Jake at a Double Diamond machine on the next row and got his attention. With a forlorn look on his face he was methodically pressing the spin button. Obviously it wasn't producing the results he wanted. Waving him over to me, he left his machine and came over to us. I turned to Kathy and asked for a favor.

"I told Jake here I would get him your autograph. Do you mind?"

"Anything for you Deb," she said with a broad smile.

She sprang to her feet announcing, "Does anyone have a pen I could use?"

At least four people standing by thrust pens in her face. To which Kathy laughingly declared, "I only need one, kids."

Happily she scrawled her name on the Cabaret playbill and handed it to Jake. Proudly he held it up for Jennifer to see. Soon Kathy had a crowd around her, and she was busy signing autographs. She autographed napkins, tickets, and assorted scraps of paper for the players crowded around her. It seemed she never left the stage. I didn't think she had planned on it, but the way she was laughing and carrying on, she didn't seem to mind it. After all, she must have been used to the attention by now.

Kathy hung around and played a while longer. Her assistant, Tom, kept handing her hundred dollar bills. She didn't win any big jackpots that I saw, but I knew she was having a good time, and it was on her terms. When he ran out, she stood up, hugged me goodbye and waved goodbye to all the rest. That was a great night that I will always remember.

Debbie Tosun Kilday

Two people that noticed me at the casino were two brothers from Yugoslavia. They were twins in their late 70's and did everything together. They frequented the casino about three times a week, mostly on weekends. They drank the same mixed drinks, played the same slot machines and seemed to talk at the same time when speaking. I had never encountered twins like this before. They were both friendly and smiley people. They also had a story to tell.

They were born in war-torn Yugoslavia and had suffered living in conflict and being dominated by others trying to take over their country. They told me of the night they both left Yugoslavia and came to the United States. They never looked back but always looked forward to the future. They would watch me play the slot machines to see if they could learn what tricks I was using to win so much. I always told them I wasn't playing any tricks to win. I just played the machines like everyone else. They never believed me when I told them there was no magic involved. They always wanted to play the machines I would sit down at and would sometimes beg me to relinquish my seat for them to have a chance to win. I always wanted them to win on their own but they never seemed too.

After getting to know them I would let them play with my money and whatever they won I let them keep and split the winnings. It was a game I think I played for my own benefit to get rid of some of the money. I felt burdened at times seeing how desperate others were, hoping they had won instead of me. Like I said earlier, the money didn't seem real while at the casino. At times I felt pressured when I would see the faces of others, desperate, hungry and wanting. I had always suffered

66

and never had any money and knew what it felt like. I didn't want that for others and tried to help the people I knew as much as I could.

8 – How Do I Act Like I Am Entitled?

My head was still reeling from all of the activity of the past few weeks. Now Mike and I were going to the casino at least four times a week. More and more people just seemed to gravitate to where I was. Nellie and I had become an inspiration of sorts for the other slot players. No matter what we played the two of us just seemed to win more than anyone else. We were putting on a show. Nellie did admit to me that when she was playing alone she did not win as much as when I was around. I seemed to be her lucky charm as she called me. At first I would never have believed it but now I couldn't seem to deny it.

There was a new couple that started hanging out with us. They were in their late sixties. Their names were Tru and Don. Tru was a nurse and Don a cop. Both of them always smiled whether they were winning or losing. Tru was very tall with a slim figure and always wore either a skirt or a dress. She wore her long bright red hair in a pony tail most of the time draped over one shoulder. Don was a tall burly looking guy with straight shoulder length blonde hair and always wore a leather vest no matter what the rest of his outfit was. Both of them were chain smokers. Looking at the two of them made me think they must have been flower children at Woodstock back in 1969. Neither looked like the typical nurse or cop. Tru and Don told us that they had met at the casino late one night while each was eating dinner alone at the Sunburst Buffet. After Don asked Tru if she wanted to join him so they wouldn't have to eat alone, they sat and began to talk. Tru had three children, two boys and a girl and Don had two children, two girls from their previous marriages. To each other's surprise they both lived in the same town of Suffield, Connecticut. Another thing they had in common was both Tru and Don had lost their spouse to cancer. Tru confided in me that was the main reason they got together. Their relationship grew from there.

The way she explained it, "We each knew the pain the other was feeling and instantly connected. We fell in love and got married five months later right here in the ballroom and we are never apart or feeling alone now."

Don added, "Our children are all grown up, married with children of their own now. If we aren't working we are either watching the grandchildren or here playing the slots."

This was such a feel good story to hear. Tru and Don made the rest of us feel good just looking at them smiling and gazing into each other's eyes. They held hands while each played their slot machine. At times Tru would sit across Don's lap while playing. There were times they were told by an attendant to go get a hotel room. Both of them would get a kick out of that. Even though they were in their sixties they looked and acted like teenagers. Tru and Don exchanged e-mail and phone numbers with Mike and I so we could keep in touch when we weren't at the casino.

Tru asked me, "Being you win so much money so often, do you have a host yet?"

I shook my head. "I don't... what is a host?"

Debbie Tosun Kilday

She gave me a sideways glance like she couldn't believe what she was hearing. "You're letting all of this winning go to waste."

Tru put her arm around me like she was giving me motherly advice. "A casino host caters to your needs while visiting the casino. You can ask your host for things like complimentary dinner reservations, room reservations, special event tickets, concert tickets, etc."

"I feel funny asking people for favors or things. I don't think I could do it." I replied.

"You should ask for a host right away because you are entitled to it. You earned the right by playing and winning so much." It almost sounded like a command.

After Tru said that to me I got to thinking that I couldn't feel right about asking or demanding anything from anyone because it just was not a part of my nature. Usually I was the one people asked things of, not the other way around. While I was sitting there playing my slot machine and contemplating all these ideas suddenly I looked at the machine I was playing and saw the red seven in the third position on the far right. A few spins later my machine hit another jackpot. This time I had won $2,000. I almost jumped up off my seat because just as the machine had won the jackpot, someone was putting their hand on my right shoulder. As I turned around, standing there was a handsome young man with jet black hair and bright blue eyes. I felt the urge to jump into his arms, but restrained myself. He was dressed in a very expensive navy blue, three piece suit. I couldn't take my eyes off of him.

The gorgeous creature spoke. "Hi my name is Cash. I was looking at your records and found you do not have your own host and you should with the way you win money. If you agree I would like to take the job of being your host." He extended his hand and I pressed my hand against his.

Immediately after coming back down to Earth, I replied with a coy smile, "Sure you can be my host."

In the back of my mind I was thinking two things. *First I was thinking that Cash had to be a fake name. Second how did I get this lucky to have a host as handsome as this? Had I been transported to an alternate reality?*

Cash said, "Just contact me anytime if you want to see a concert, have dinner at Todd English's Tuscany or any of our other fine restaurants, see a show, go to the spa, etc. Here's my card."

He extended his hand and gently placed his card in my hand. I looked over at Nellie and Tru to see them swooning helplessly in their seats. They were envious that I was getting this guy as my host and they weren't.

"Thank you, Cash." I even batted an eyelash at him, and he responded with a smile. I tried not to act like a person that didn't know what they wanted.

"There are some concerts coming up that I might be interested in. I will give you a call once I look at the concert schedule." I slipped his card into the zippered pouch in my pocketbook where I kept the important things I didn't want to lose.

"I'll be waiting", he said seductively. With that he strolled around the bank of slot machines and was gone as silently as he came. I noticed all of the women playing in the row of slot machines had their eyes fixed on him as he departed.

Tru and Nellie were melting in their seats. They seemed frozen in time, their fingers poised above the spin buttons on their machines. Everything had stopped while Cash was there. I wasn't hearing any of the normal slot machines clicks, buzzes, or music while Cash was speaking to me. The silence was deafening. The spell was broken when two slot attendants came to pay me for the $2000 jackpot. It had slipped my mind that I was waiting to be paid for my win. I held out my hand. They counted out the crisp $100 bills into my hand, and I gave them a generous tip.

After they left, Tru broke the silence. "Now that's what I call a host. I want one of those."

Nellie nodded in agreement, "You're one lucky shit."

Weeks had passed. I was unstoppable it seemed. Mike and I spent more time at the casino than at home. We stayed in my complementary room, ate complementary food, and attended complementary concerts. Our lives were being 'comped' every time we turned around. That was the term high rollers used to describe the freebies the casino rewarded their favorite players with.

Mike had to go to work but I didn't have any work to go home for. Even though I was disabled I could sit and play a slot machine. I was now free to enjoy something in life instead of dwelling on the negativity of the outside 'real' world.

My host Cash was now hearing from me on a daily basis. I was asking for things and getting them. I was fast becoming someone that knew exactly what they wanted and was no longer afraid to ask for it. I marveled at how ingrained my behavior had been, and how quickly it could change. It was funny how things changed. In the past I was always unable to accept a simple gift from anyone. What I didn't comprehend was:

there is no reason why you should not accept a gift or gifts from people if they are being offered honestly and freely.

It all went back to my upbringing. Indirectly I was made to feel that I was somehow a substandard human being, basically not deserving. If I did not suffer enough I did not deserve to be happy or have fun. If I did not earn it according to someone else's standards, I was made to feel guilty and would stop myself from any enjoyment. With the help of my new host Cash and my new friends at the casino, I learned it was okay to express your needs verbally to others. Who better than you would know what your wants or needs were? For the first time in fifty years, I was learning to express myself, and it was carrying over into all different facets of my life. I was getting exactly what I asked for when I asked for it. I also realized something else: *there is always hope for anyone to get what their heart desires. They just had to be open to new experiences.*

Another friend I had made at Mohegan Sun was a nurse in her mid-fifties by the name of Dee. Dee always looked sad every time I saw her. She cared for the elderly at a local nursing home and when not working she cared for her elderly parents that she lived with. She always was neatly dressed and even when not working wore her long blonde hair coiled into a bun on top of her head. She would arrive at the casino alone as did I. Sometimes she would come before work and sometimes after working. Most of the time she was wearing her nurse's uniform because she had no time to change into street clothes.

At first she wasn't friendly to me. She would sit down at a slot machine, and order a drink even if it was early morning. Then she would light up a cigarette. This was her routine. She would try to avoid eye contact with other people so they would not try to talk to her. Until this one particular day, I never bothered her. I looked over at her and I could tell she had been crying. I should have just left her alone but I felt compelled to offer the hand of friendship to her.

I started out by saying, "Hi, I just want to tell you that I am a good listener if you ever need anyone to talk to or just a friend to share anything, anything at all with."

At first she ignored me even though I knew she had heard me. About ten minutes later though she burst into tears, turned to me and said, "Yes I could use a friend right now."

"Okay. I'm Debbie, what's your name?"

She responded, "Dee."

"Do you want to go into the lounge to talk where it is less noisy?" I asked.

Not even looking up she shook her head yes. I cashed out of my machine and she cashed out of hers. We both got up and started walking over to the VIP Sachem Lounge. After we sat down across from each other at one of the tables, I waited until she started talking first.

Dee turned to me and said, "I want to thank you for two things. First, for not bothering me all this time I have sat here wanting to be left alone; second, for not leaving me alone today because I really could use a friend—Thanks."

This was the first time I saw anything that resembled a smile from her. We went into the lounge and sat across from each other on a set of blue plush velvet couches.

Dee took a deep breath and began. "As you can guess, I am a nurse. I have been a nurse for a long, long time and have seen many people suffering from all kinds of dread diseases. It is part of my profession and most of the time I look past the individuals as people and instead think of each of them as just a case number. You have to look at them that way or you would end up having a nervous breakdown."

"So what happened last night that would upset you so much?" I inquired.

Dee paused to gather her thoughts. "Well, one of the patients that has been a resident in the nursing home where I work for over ten years passed away last night. He didn't have any family that we knew of at all. There were no relatives listed on his paperwork when he first arrived. No one ever visited him in the last ten years except for this one friend of his that he had, but he died three years ago and there hasn't been anyone visiting him since. He used to tell all the other nurses and even the doctors that I had adopted him as my Uncle Joe and that he thought of me as a daughter. About five years ago Joe told me that one day he would repay me for my kindness and compassion I showed him. Last night when I came in for my shift I knew he was dying. I stayed with him at his side until he passed. I asked the other nurses if they would cover my other patients for me. My boss called me into the office before I left work this morning. I asked her why she was calling me in. She told me that I was listed as Joe's only relative on his paperwork. Then my boss told me that I would be contacted by Joe's attorney as Joe had left me a large sum of money. All of the years I had cared for Joe he never told me that he had named me as his beneficiary. I never really knew any personal details about him before he entered the nursing home. He had told me once that his wife and daughter had died in a car accident and that he had survived it but wished he hadn't. That was the only personal history on Joe. No other relatives were listed besides me."

Dee started crying again. I got up and sat down next to her and let her lean on me as she wept quietly trying not to let the other patrons notice her. From that day on Dee and I became good friends. As it turned out Dee told me at a later date she inherited around $250,000 from Joe's estate. After that first encounter with Dee she never ignored me again. She even became friends with Nellie after I introduced the two of them. She always kept her guard up around most other people though.

There were several other people that I became friends with while playing slot machines. The reason we met was because of our mutual love of playing the Bally's Bonus Times machines. They were machines that would win over and over again. Most people would win smaller amounts of five hundred dollars or less. The money won would keep everyone playing for hours and hours. It was good for us and also for the casino to have regulars playing like that.

One of these regulars was a woman by the name of Aqua. She was proud of the fact that her parents had given her such an unusual name. She would brag about her name every chance she could. Aqua was in her late eighty's but looked like she was in her sixties. She always wore dresses that were so neatly pressed. She had permed silver white hair cut to her jaw line. Her big bright blue eyes were striking. I knew that she must have been beautiful all of her life.

She told me that she loved coming to the casino and she was able to because she was a wealthy widow. She had been married four times and she told me that she never married for love only for money. I asked her if she had ever been in love and she answered yes. She told me of a man she had met while in her early forties. He was a laborer as she put it. She was married at the time and so was he. She told me that she had never experienced falling in love before and was immediately drawn to him. She had tried to fight her feelings for this man but it was a fight neither she nor he would win. She was quite graphic in her description to me about the first night they made love. Her husband at the time was always working at his office and hardly ever at home. The laborer was an employee of her husband.

One night she invited this man to come into the house for a drink after he had been hard at work outside at her estate all day. At first he told her that he should be getting home to his wife but Aqua convinced him that just one friendly drink wouldn't take much time. He agreed and came into the house. He sat on the sofa and she sat nearby in an armchair. She told me that he couldn't keep his eyes off of her and he was looking at her body while taking sips of his drink. At first they made small conversation about practically nothing. Then when she least expected it he told Aqua that he had tried to overlook his feelings for her all this time. But it was now getting impossible for him to be near her without wanting to take her in his arms and make mad passionate love to her right there on the sofa.

Debbie Tosun Kilday

She told me that all the while she had been
fantasizing about him and how she wished to be in his
arms. It was like the two of them were thinking the
same thoughts. She got up off of the armchair and while
walking towards him on the sofa she started to undo the
buttons on the front of her dress one by one. He
immediately got up to meet her halfway, pressed his
body against hers and then pulling her tighter,
surrounded her open mouth with his. They kissed with
such a passion that they both knew at that moment
there would be no denying their feelings for each other
any longer.

I found it hard to listen to her stories of their
passionate lovemaking without thinking about myself in
present times. I too have had that kind of passion in my
life but it had been a long time since and I missed
experiencing those kinds of feelings. Aqua taught me
that you should not deny your passions concerning
everything you do in life. Here she was, still so vibrant
in her late eighties. I hoped that I would be like her
when I got older.

This passionate love affair did produce Aqua's only
child, a son. Her husband at the time accepted the child
and claimed him as his own so as to not draw attention
to his wife's affair. Her husband was first and always a
business man Aqua told me. As her husband at the
time put it, "That kind of thing getting out in society is
not good for my business so it will not go outside this
house." Aqua's lover also died at a young age. She told
me that was the one and only time she felt real love in
her life. I met Aqua's son a few times while at the
casino. He was a grown man but acted like a little rich
boy. He depended on his mother and her money. He

78

didn't have a job, and didn't need one but he had no drive to accomplish anything in his own life it seemed. I admired her but pitied him. I wondered how such a strong woman could have such a son of weak character.

A casino friend by the name of Tony was introduced to me by my friend Nellie. Tony was a client of Nellie's. Nellie had prepared Tony's taxes for years and both he and his wife were good friends. Tony was a local small business owner. He ran a machine shop that made parts for commercial airplanes. I really liked Tony and his wife Mary. Whenever they saw me at the casino they would make sure they stopped to say hello and spend some time talking to me.

They were always taking cruises to different exotic locations around the world. When they would meet up with me at the casino they would tell me of their adventures. Sometimes Nellie, Mike and I would go to the lounge to grab a bite to eat with Tony and his wife Mary. They thoroughly enjoyed life and took advantage of all the opportunities available to them. The best way to describe Tony if you had never met him before would be to describe him as a person with a strong lust for life and living. His wife had the same attitude as him.

I forgot to mention that Tony was bound to a wheelchair since a car accident that left him paralyzed from the waist down years earlier. Tony was one of those inspirational people that everyone could learn a lesson from. He always looked towards the future and was not afraid to enjoy what life had to offer. He made the best he could out of the hand he had been dealt by life. After getting to know Tony I almost forgot he was bound to that chair. It was a tool to help him get around

Debbie Tosun Kilday

but it did not define who he was. I admired him for his lust for life.

There were a total of eighty people that I knew by name at the casino. I was there so frequently everyone got to know me and I got to know them. Some shared things about themselves and some didn't. Whether they told them or not, they all had stories to tell. In my opinion, all of them were good people. I never would have met any of them if it had not been for the fact that I started going to the casino. I was glad I got to meet all of them. *It is my belief that there is a reason for everything that happens whether you realized it or not. It is best to be open by embracing new experiences.*

9 - The High Roller Coaster Ride

After winning close to $200,000 within a few months time I decided it was time to go back to the 'Pit' and explore the high roller areas of the casino. Dollar machines were no longer giving me satisfaction. I was meeting lots of new people while still keeping my dear friends Nellie, Mitch, Mindy, Mark, Tru and Don close. Nellie was my closest friend. All of the people I was meeting had more suffering in their lives than most and had come to the casino to seek refuge and escape from it if only for a little while. The casino certainly was a distraction from most people's everyday lives.

One particular night Mike and I had complimentary tickets to see Rod Stewart in concert. He was playing in the arena. We both love all kinds of music but we were excited to be seeing a rock legend like Rod Stewart. Before the show we would be meeting him in person backstage. My host Cash had arranged the whole thing. Upon arriving at the casino we just happened to walk in at the same exact time as Mitch and his wife. We had both used the valet to park. Mike and I had never met Mitch's wife before so I was looking forward to it. Mitch's wife was a gorgeous long legged blonde and she was dressed like a celebrity. She wore a silver sequined dress with matching high heeled stiletto shoes. I guess with all of Mitch's player's club points and her spending all that time at the spa and the shops in the casino mall

Debbie Tosun Kilday

buying clothes and jewelry, this was a good reason why we had never met her before.

Mitch saw Mike and I and immediately headed towards us to introduce us to her.

Mitch said, "Hey Mike and Deb, this is Sarah.

Sarah shyly smiled and said, "Hi."

Before we could get any conversation going a crowd of women started running towards us yelling, "Oh my God, there's Rod Stewart."

I had seen Mitch so often while playing at the casino that I had forgotten just how much he resembled Rod Stewart. The crowd had mistaken him for the real celebrity. Mike and I just had to laugh out loud while Mitch tried to fend off his temporary fans. They had gathered around him and were shoving pens and pieces of paper to sign in his face. Some women were tugging at his clothes. I supposed in the hopes they could rip them off.

All the while Mitch kept saying "I'm not Rod. I just look like him".

Sarah on the other hand seemed to like all the attention. She hung onto her man so he wouldn't be swept away into the crowd. Finally one of the women heard him above the confused clamor. "How come you don't have an English accent, Rod?"

"Because I'm not Rod Stewart—I'm from Boston." He shot back.

Finally the crowd recognized their mistake and quickly dispersed. Mike put his arm on Mitch's shoulder. "We could set you up a table in Spin Street for after the show." Mitch eyed him suspiciously then burst out laughing.

"I wonder if other used car dealers have this problem."

They looked each in the eye and said "Nah" in unison.

While Mitch adjusted his clothing he asked, "Do you want to join us for dinner at Tuscany?" He cast a side glance at Sarah to see if she approved.

She batted her eyelashes seductively and said, "Please join us".

Mike and I immediately said, "Yes, let's do it."

Todd English's Tuscany Restaurant was one of the classiest restaurants at Mohegan Sun. Always had good food and an atmosphere to go with it. Mike and I usually ate in the VIP lounge mostly because I was always playing a slot machine and Nellie didn't like going into a restaurant and eating alone. The VIP lounge was more private and casual in seating.

As we were passing through the hotel lobby on our way to Tuscany, I turned to Mitch. "Should we include Nellie in our dinner plans?"

Mitch thought for a moment, then responded, "Why not?"

I called Nellie on her cell phone to ask her if she would go to dinner with us. She answered her phone sounding happy for a change. She was giggling which was not like the Nellie we hung out with. I put her on the speaker phone so we could all hear.

Nellie asked, "Can I bring someone along with me?"

"I guess so," I replied, then hung up.

Mitch seemed taken back a little. "Who is she talking about?"

I shrugged my shoulders. "I don't know but we will all find out shortly".

Debbie Tosun Kilday

As we met up with Nellie she was walking and giggling alongside a smiling shaggy grey haired guy holding a drink in one hand while the other hand was around her waist. I had never seen him around the casino floor before.

Nellie said, "Hi guys this is John."

As we introduced ourselves to John, he checked each one of us out briefly, but his gaze always returned to Nellie. It was hard for the rest of us to ignore how intent his focus was on her.

Todd English's Tuscany restaurant had a bar and a lounge situated in front of it. Behind the bar rose a wall of rock shaped into a waterfall which the Mohegan Tribe called Taughannick Falls. The water poured out of a hole in the wall, and cascaded down into a pool below. The restaurant stood at the edge of the shopping mall which was situated between two casinos, the Casino of the Earth and the Casino of the Sky. Out in front of Tuscany near the escalators was a pool of water which patrons used as a wishing well. It was full of coins of all denominations that glittered in the bright lights of the shopping mall. The lighting was accentuated by the flash of cameras all around the wishing well, and the hand blown glass sculpture in colors of blue, silver, and clear glass that rose out of it. The twisted glass shapes pointed outward in all directions from the center of the sculpture. Patrons liked to snap pictures of each other in front of the artwork.

We gathered on the steps of the bridge walkway that led into the restaurant. We then casually strolled across into the restaurant together with Mitch and Sarah leading the way. At the reception desk, Mitch said to the receptionist "There will be four others joining us for dinner."

She cast a glance back toward the maitre d' and he nodded his approval. "That will be no problem, sir."

She grabbed a handful of leather-bound black menus and motioned, "This way please."

As we sat down I noticed that John was fawning over Nellie and she loved every minute of it. Usually Nellie was very apprehensive when a man even tried to strike up a conversation with her, but Nellie didn't seem to mind John's advances at all. I wondered why, but also felt a little protective of Nellie.

"How do you know each other?" I inquired.

John said, "I just met her today while playing a slot machine next to her."

"Do you come here a lot?"

"Whenever I can get away from my business," John continued. He went on to note that he was from West Springfield, Massachusetts and was in manufacturing. He admitted he was single, lived with and cared for his elderly mother. Then he dropped a bombshell.

"I had never met anyone I ever thought about getting serious with until today." His eyes were riveted on Nellie. It almost sounded like a wedding proposal. The rest of us tried not to act surprised but we were shocked.

Nellie started giggling and then playfully told John to, "Fuck off."

John then took her hand in his and turning to us said, "Isn't she the most gorgeous creature you ever laid your eyes on?"

Then he added, "I love it when she talks dirty like that."

We all burst out laughing. John was a likable Irish fellow who drank quite a bit. The glass in front of him always seemed to be half-empty because he had it filled so often. I hoped it wasn't the beer talking when he professed his undying love for Nellie.

After dinner we went to meet the real Rod Stewart before his show. I had made arrangements with my host, Cash, for Mike and I to do a 'meet and greet' with Rod Stewart before his show. Meet and greet was a program Mohegan Sun reserved for its high rollers. I used one of the house phones to call my host to ask him if all six of us could meet Rod Stewart before the concert. Cash told me it was not a problem. Cash never denied any of my requests.

I was a little nervous to meet Rod Stewart being he was a big rock and roll star. As soon as we walked into the waiting room outside his dressing room Rod Stewart ran towards Mitch embracing him with a big hug saying, "I didn't know I had a twin brother here." We all laughed heartily. That kind of broke the ice.

Rod, a notorious ladies' man in his younger days, looked Sarah up and down. "Who is this beautiful young lady?"

Sarah swooned. Rod took her by the hand and gently twirled her around. She was dizzy already and fell back into his arms. This was exactly what you would expect from Rod Stewart. It was like he was warming up before he performed his act on stage.

When Rod tired of twirling Sarah around, he gave her a peck on the cheek. She giggled nervously. Sensing that the other women were feeling left out; Rod pecked each one of them on the cheek in turn, me, then Nellie.

After satisfying the ladies, Rod grinned, very pleased with himself.

"Old habits die hard. Don't they Rod?" Mike noted.

Rod laughed and slapped Mike on the back. "That's what we do it for. Don't we?" Then he winked at Mike, Mitch and John so the ladies would see.

Not waiting for an answer, he added, "I'm sorry to dash off but the show must go on." He gave us an abbreviated bow, and said "It was a pleasure to meet you. Enjoy the show." Then he spun around and rushed back toward the dressing rooms, his road manager and security guards in tow. We watched Rod and his entourage disappear into the backstage area that encircled the Mohegan Sun arena.

We only had a few minutes with him but it was worth it. Cash turned to me. "Was it all that you expected?"

"And more," I returned, "Thank you."

Cash nodded in agreement. "I thought so too."

He and the Mohegan Sun security guards escorted us out of the reception room into the arena to our seats in the Mohegan Sun Arena. They put us in the first section next to center stage, row C. It wasn't the first row but it was close enough. I looked around the arena. It was almost a packed house. Even the cheap seats on the nose-bleed level were mostly filled. The rolling electronic marquee around the arena was silently announcing the acts that were coming in the near future. The words Aerosmith, Maroon Five, Reba Macintyre and Bon Jovi crawled across the rolling marquee. Because their arena held about 10,000 people they could attract the biggest names in the music business. We saw as many of them as we could, courtesy of my host Cash. As long as I remained a high roller, the complimentary tickets for the big-name shows kept coming my way.

When the house lights began to dim, we knew the show was about to start. From the moment Rod walked out on stage, we saw he was primed to do a great show. The cheering of the crowd began the moment he walked out on stage and it was clear he graciously accepted the adulation. The show that Rod Stewart put on dazzled the senses. Being the ultimate showman, the visual effects on the screen behind him, and the songs he chose in his set were timed perfectly. He performed all of his hits. While watching him perform on stage, I thought, *He really is so sexy especially seeing him performing in person.* The excitement of the crowd coupled with the energy Rod infused as a performer made it an exciting night.

After the show Mitch said he was going up with Sarah to their room but maybe would see us downstairs later on. We headed into the Sky Casino with Nellie and John. John sat right next to Nellie whispering sweet nothings in her ear as he leaned towards her. Nellie was still giggling like a school girl. John ordered another drink and then another. Nellie was not much of a drinker and asked the waitress for a bottle of water. We felt like we were interrupting something being Nellie and John looked so involved together. They were so engrossed in each other they didn't even see what was going on around them. Seeing that, Mike and I didn't stay long and went up to our own room soon after.

The next day I had to call Nellie right away to find out what happened if anything between her and John the night before. Nellie answered her phone knowing it would be me asking those questions. Nellie began by telling me that John was the first person since her husband that even got her attention as far as her considering that something might come of it. She tried to resist his advances but she decided she really didn't want to.

The fact that he drank a lot of alcohol did bother her though. He was a kind and gentle man and the thing that made her take notice was the fact that he was so attentive to her and such a romantic. She didn't sleep with him that first night because he didn't ask her to. She would have considered it if he had but, he was too much of a gentleman was how she explained it.

We decided we would meet Nellie downstairs for breakfast at Fidelia's Restaurant in an hour. When we arrived an hour later John was with her again. He had called her after I had and asked if he could take her to breakfast. John was one of the nicest guys I had ever met. He told us about himself while we were waiting for the waitress to come and take our orders. He lived in Massachusetts and took care of his ailing mother who had a stroke two years prior. He had never been married or as he put it, "Yet".

He owned his own manufacturing business making brass cabinet hardware. He worked alone except when he got really busy, he would hire temps to help with the workload. I wondered how this guy could not be married all this time. I tried to find something wrong with him but couldn't. He really was a great guy. I was happy Nellie found someone to be with and maybe find some happiness in her life.

Over the next few weeks Mike and I would meet Nellie at the casino as we always did but now John would join us too. Both Mike and I became close friends with him. We met his only sister one night that was visiting from Florida. Her name was Kim. She had a slight build, wavy dirty blonde hair and was much younger than John. She was married and had three kids. She was very protective of her brother John but after getting to know Nellie she embraced her as one of her own. I came to find out John was very well off financially; so it made sense why his sister was protective of him.

While playing two Blazing Sevens slot machines next to me, John confided. "I'm totally in love with her." It was obvious he meant Nellie.

"Have you told Nellie about this?"

"Not yet. I wanted to know what you thought first... Should I tell her?"

I wanted to be straight with him because Nellie had already talked to me about her feelings for John. By her own admission the idea of having a new love relationship scared her to death. She was still a little fragile. Her husband's early death had thrown her for a loop. It had been several years and she still hadn't recovered from the shock yet. She did her best to hide it, but it continued to haunt her.

I looked John in the eye. "I want to be honest with you John. I can't be any happier for you and Nellie. The two of you finding each other like you did is amazing. I do have to say though that your excessive drinking does not sit well with Nellie. If you really want to have a serious relationship with her you better cut down on the drinking. Nellie has to know that what you feel for her is real without the alcohol."

John hung his head a bit then straightened up and looked me in the eye. "Deb, I know this myself. Being by myself all these years, being single, taking care of my Mom, I know I have been drinking to occupy myself or to forget about how lonely I am."

He went on to say, "I will do anything for that girl. I know I haven't known her that long but Deb, I'm telling you, I am totally in love with her."

Looking into his eyes I knew he was telling the truth. From that night on whenever I saw John and Nellie together John was not drinking as much. Occasionally he would have a beer or two but I didn't see him drinking any hard liquor like when we had first met him. He was trying hard to be the kind of man Nellie expected him to be like he had said. It made me feel happy for Nellie.

My casino home became a network of friends that were like my family. All the while my real family didn't much bother with me unless they wanted to be treated by me to all the activities the casino offered. I found out that I was being talked about behind my back concerning my casino activity. My family wasn't happy about all the money I was winning at the casino even though they did not turn down all those concert tickets, hotel rooms, spa visits, dinners, shopping, etc. In fact they had no problem asking me for all those perks.

At a family function I was cornered. I was asked directly as to whom I would be leaving all that money to, just in case something were to happen to me. I guessed some things never changed. The complex thing we called 'human nature' was rearing its ugly head. I felt used and abused by my relatives jealousy but yet I wanted to think the best of them. I saw the facts but

Debbie Tosun Kilday

chose to ignore them. Everyone wanted to be loved and nurtured by their family. Usually when you had no one else in your life you counted on family to always be there. The money I was winning didn't make me feel happy because of how I was being treated by family and some friends. Besides treating family members to all the casino perks I even offered to give them cash money. They grabbed the money but still were not treating me fairly.

At one huge gathering of family members for one of their birthdays, we were all sitting eating cake when one of them started talking about how gamblers are such low life degenerates and how they had no respect for them. I tried to stay silent but I knew I couldn't after hearing a remark like that in my presence.

I asked, "Are you referring to me?"

In unison they all said, "Yes".

Then all of the others started one by one to attack me verbally calling me names. I got up and left the gathering feeling hurt and betrayed. After that night I kept my guard up while in their presence. In fact I made a conscious effort to limit the number of times I saw any of them.

10 – Here Comes the Tax Man

This may sound like a strange thing to say but all the while playing slot machines and winning taxable amounts and collecting all of those W2G slips I was always asked by the attendants if I wanted any federal or state taxes taken out of my wins and I always said no. Why I always said no, I am not sure. I guess I just did not think about it. Late one night I was playing slot machines in the Pit alongside my friend Mark.

Mark would always ask me, "Do you know any young women you can introduce me to?"

I didn't so I would say to him, "Don't worry Mark, one of these days you will meet your dream girl; just be a little more patient."

A guy I had never seen before came and sat down at a Double Diamond machine on the other side of me. I tried not to really focus on him but I could see out of the corner of my eye that he was watching me intently instead of looking or paying attention to his own machine. He looked like a studious type of person. His horn-rimmed eyeglasses protruded from an egg-shaped head which at first glance made me think of the character George Costanza of Seinfeld, only with a thick head of hair.

I was playing a two coin, $5, Double Blazing Seven's, quick hit machine where if you got three quick hit symbols to come up on the screen in any order you

Debbie Tosun Kilday

would win the progressive jackpot which in this case was around $5000 dollars. All of the quick hit machines played basically the same. The difference was if you were playing a dollar or a five dollar denomination machine. I knew the machine was going to hit soon because of what I was seeing on the screen. Minutes before I had seen what I like to call the crisscross. From left to right looking at the face of the machine I saw the red blazing seven in the upper left hand corner, one on the line, and one in the lower left hand corner. A few spins later I saw the reverse. When looking left to right at the face of the machine I saw the red blazing seven in the lower left hand corner, one on the line, and one in the upper right hand corner. I knew from past experience: *when you see this, it is an indication that the machine is getting ready to pay out the progressive jackpot amount.*

I had already played in around eight hundred dollars into the machine when Mark turned to me and said, "My curfew has arrived. I have to get up early tomorrow and meet with some clients. I'm calling it a night."

I said, "Take it easy driving home and call me if you need company next time you are here."

Mark thanked me, got up and left.

As soon as Mark was out of sight the guy playing next to me said, "You look like you come here often. Do you win often too?"

I knew I couldn't really ignore the guy but I was thinking it was none of his business. I shrugged my shoulders thinking that should be answer enough, hoping he wouldn't ask anything further. At that moment I hit the progressive jackpot but instead of the three quick hits being scattered in different places on

94

the face of the machine they were lined up right on the line straight across. When that happened, which was rather rare, it meant that you not only won the progressive amount shown at the top of the machine. It meant I had just won $50,000. Three quick hits on the line plus the progressive $5,080 amount was shown at the top. I was shocked at this outcome but not as shocked as I would be in the next second.

The guy next to me said, "Nice win, but let me just say that you better take that federal and state tax out when the attendant comes around."

In my face, he thrust a business card which read Federal Tax Investigator. At first I thought this must be a joke but he didn't look like he was laughing. He was dead serious. A feeling of foreboding came over me making me wonder what was going to happen to me next.

He went on to say, "I was sent here to monitor you and your play tonight. Let's just say that you are a person of interest."

At that moment thoughts raced through my head of all the winnings and all the money given away to others. Then I calmed down thinking that I had only played since last July and it was now February of the next year. I had not yet done the taxes for the past year and had until April, 15th. There was still time.

The next thought that came into my head was *how could I have forgotten about the tax implications winning all this money? Am I a stupid idiot or just living in my own dream world the last couple of months? Maybe I am both.*

Then the guy spoke again. "Just a friendly warning."

Debbie Tosun Kilday

It didn't sound so friendly; more like the calm before the storm. A hurricane was chugging up the coast, and it was about to make landfall. I wanted to escape but I couldn't just walk away at that moment. I had to wait until I collected my money. The first name on his business card read 'Clark' but I will call him only by the name, 'Taxman'.

Taxman repeated, "I was sent here to monitor you but don't worry. I also play here myself as you are witnessing tonight."

I didn't know what to make of this 'Taxman' guy. The attendant came over at that point and said, "That is a fantastic win, Deborah. Will you be taking state and federal taxes out tonight?"

In my defiance and my total dislike for people telling me what I can and cannot do I wanted to say, *Yes, I most definitely will be taking out the state taxes but not the federal*. Taxman smiled at me with his beady little eyes. His bushy eyebrows arched and he brushed away his salt and pepper bangs from his forehead waiting to hear my answer to the attendant.

I, of course, gave into the system. "Take out the federal and state taxes, please".

As he was leaving he said, "You will be hearing from me soon." Then he got up and left the 'Pit'.

In early March I made an appointment to do our income taxes. I had been going to the same woman for the last sixteen years. I will call her 'Tax Lady' for lack of a better title. She was always nice to me and talked to me about our cats being she was a cat lover herself. I loved my tax lady but all that was about to change. I brought all of our tax stuff to drop off to her and she looked at it piece by piece as she usually did before I would leave it with her. She accounted for the interest we had paid in for our mortgage, looked at Mike's statement of income and mine too.

"Well you seem to have everything here all in order."

I said to her, "Well, I have some new stuff to add this year."

I then took out an 8 ½" X 11" envelope stuffed almost to the bursting point, filled with W2G slips from the casino taxable wins. Tax Lady's usual smiley face turned sour as she looked at me. She started looking at the W2G slips one by one in silence.

"You started gambling and going to a casino?"

I said, "Yes." It felt like an admission of guilt.

She thumbed through the pile of W2G slips in front of her. "And by the looks of all these W2G slips you won all this money just playing slot machines?"

"Yes", I said, "why do you ask? I know I have won an incredible amount of money there in a short time. It seems unreal to me too."

Then Tax Lady dropped the bomb, "I will do your taxes this year because I already committed to doing them, but next year find someone else."

I had a distressed, puzzled look on my face I was sure and then asked her, "Why?"

"I'll tell you why Debbie. I thought that you were one of the most decent people I got to know while doing your taxes all these years. Now you go and become a degenerate gambler. I want nothing to do with your kind of person and Mike should divorce you if he is smart."

I was in shock. "What the Hell is going on here? I went to a casino, won money and now I am a degenerate? Even if I had lost money I still am not a degenerate; Gambler yes, degenerate no."

Debbie Tosun Kilday

That year Tax Lady did our taxes for the last time. She wasn't nice about it either. I suspected we ended up paying more taxes than we actually owed. Also her fee for doing our taxes went from two hundred fifty dollars to nine hundred eighty dollars. At the end of the torture from Tax Lady I ended up having to dish out close to one hundred and twenty four thousand dollars in taxes. This was depressing to say the least.

I was the same Debbie I always was but now I was also labeled a gambler. In the eyes of society that made people think differently about who I was. Now they didn't just see me and judge me for the person I was but also judged me for where I went. As a person that frequented the casino I was put in a category as someone that lived a degenerate lifestyle or worse. I wondered how this could be. I wasn't the only person in the casino. In fact the casino was filled with thousands of people every day.

Most of the people that I met in the casino were considered upstanding citizens. I met doctors, lawyers, even tax people there. The only difference between me and all the others was I didn't lose thousands. I won them most of the time. The only explanation I could imagine was: *some people don't like to see other people win. They want to see themselves winning and everyone else losing. If they lose they want everyone else to lose too. Misery loves company.* The casino liked winners only if they could try to draw you back in to lose whatever you won. I tried not to let Tax Lady's behavior and remarks bother me but they did. This wouldn't be the last time I would hear remarks like that from others as well.

11 – Vegas Baby!

By now I was making six figures playing slot machines and I wasn't even six months into the New Year. I was completely exhausted mentally and physically just from thinking about it. At the same time I didn't want to stop playing because it was too much fun and there was too much potential money to walk away from. The real question was: *where were all my winnings?* I didn't have them.

I was comped free rooms, free meals, free concerts, free shopping so you would think I had a bank account filled with money. That was not the case. As much as I won money I spent just as much if not more at times. Not on myself but for the desires of others. Everyone wanted a piece of what I had created. I allowed it even though I knew more than half of them were just users. You would think these users were people I met at the casino but this was not the case. Most of the people that frequented the casino were like family to me. Our little group of players had mutual respect for each other.

The real users turned out to be friends I hadn't seen in years and even some long lost relatives. People wanted to live the life I was living even though they didn't want to work for it like I had. I felt like I needed a change of scenery. I was now getting invitations to all the casinos around the country. They always maintained they didn't sell your private information to others but I was thinking they must just give it away. I decided that I would check out Las Vegas and see if I knew the machines there as well as I knew the machines in Connecticut.

Thinking back I realized I was always challenging myself and looking for new adventures. There had always been a void of some sort that I recognized in myself. Growing up I was never good enough, smart enough or accomplished enough to satisfy my parents. I didn't want to stop going to the casino and playing the slots. It was something I was good at. I was really good at it. Others couldn't take that ability away from me. Yet I was still not accepted. In the case of family, some disowned me altogether.

It was the middle of June and I booked a flight for Mike and me to go to Las Vegas. Little did I know how hot it would be. That just goes to show I had not been many places in my life up to that point. The temperature in June was well over a hundred degrees every day and in the high eighties at night. Stepping into the Vegas sunshine at mid-day was like climbing into an oven. When you retreated back into the air-conditioned buildings, it was with a sunburn in record time.

If you had never been to Las Vegas all I could say was you should put it on your list of places to go. The adrenaline rush you felt when you saw the larger than life buildings, neon lights, and the lavish surroundings took your breath away. I had comped rooms, free play and headliner shows all waiting for me. All of the major casinos wanted me to stay at their resort. They were hoping to get a piece of me too.

When arriving at McCarran Airport there was a blonde woman in her mid sixties holding a sign up with my name on it. She was my limo driver. Out of all the major casinos, the Las Vegas Hilton had bothered to go the extra mile to vie for my attention. It worked. The limo was sent from the Las Vegas Hilton and that was where Mike and I were heading. I called the other hotels and told them I would take them up on their generous offers at another point in time.

As we were getting into the white stretch limo, my driver introduced herself.

"My name is Mary."

She was a Las Vegas native. "One of the few natives left," she said proudly.

As she drove us to our hotel, she told us stories of her friendship with Elvis back in the day. By the time we got to the hotel I had tears in my eyes from the stories she told me of Elvis's generosity and kindness toward everyone he met. Of anyone that has really known him I had only heard good stories about him.

"He used to come visit me when I lived with my parents. I had a few dates with him but only as a friend and not a lover. Elvis bought me and my brother our first cars which of course were Cadillacs."

It made me feel good inside to know that Elvis never forgot where he had come from. He treated others well and never put on airs. Truly he was a man of the people.

The whole city was bustling. On the strip people were on the move. It reminded me of a time when I lived on the Upper West side of New York City where things didn't start happening until midnight. The streets were filled with people. The neon signs of the different hotels and casinos flashed on and off brightly. While driving to the hotel we could see the huge Las Vegas Hilton sign from a distance.

"That sign is close to three hundred feet tall." Mary announced proudly.

When we arrived at the hotel it was close to 2am. Mary got out and opened the limo door for me and Mike. She handed Mike her business card. "If you need a ride anywhere, just give me a call."

Mike pressed a $20 bill into her hand. "I'll be waiting for your call," she added.

I was tired from the long flight but upon entering the hotel lobby, I couldn't help but be dazzled by the lobby décor. There was a huge round crystal chandelier that seemed to cover more than half of the entire ceiling. Under the lights of the chandelier was a circular geometric mosaic pattern with shades of gold and beige surrounded by an outline of black on the floor. I saw some slot machines just off of the lobby that I never had seen back East. I decided to investigate right away. I am not sure what the technical name for the machine was but it was two dollars a spin. It had a big wheel like a Wheel of Fortune machine but that was the only similarity. I put a hundred dollar bill into the machine and started playing it. After just a couple of spins it talked.

A mechanical voice said, "Wheel winner" and then beeped a couple of times. I wasn't sure what I had to do but figured it out soon enough. I had to either take the win of $500 or decide to let the wheel spin picking red or black. You could double your money if you picked the right color and landed on it. I figured what the Hell. I picked black and spun the wheel. It came up black so now I had won a thousand dollars. It didn't stop there. I could continue to try and double my money or take my win. I continued to choose black for the next five spins and kept doubling my money. I wondered if the machine was stuck on black or if I was just lucky. I decided I would choose red the next time around. Now I had accumulated close to twelve thousand dollars and if red didn't come up I would lose it all. If I won though, I would double up to twenty four thousand dollars. Thinking back now I know I was throwing all caution to the wind by taking that chance but I did it anyway. I chose red and the wheel spun and landed on red. At that point I chose to take my winnings.

When the slot attendant came, I discovered that in Las Vegas they did not take taxes out of what you won. It was your responsibility to report back to your state of origin but they did issue you a W2G slip for taxable amounts won. I realized at that very moment I was trying to escape from the situation at home but I had now created the same situation here. After being paid by the slot attendant, we decided to go up to our room to sleep for a few hours.

Later that morning I tried my luck on an old-fashioned mechanical slot machine situated in the center of the hotel lobby. It was a 10X Bally's machine. It was eight feet tall and four feet wide, big enough to be seen from anywhere on the casino floor. Because it was ancient, it played really slow. You could actually hear the reels clicking through their cycle, and each of the three reels spun slowly and revealed their results methodically, left to right. Mike refused to play it because it took so long for the reels to spin. He was too used to the electronic type of slot machine that spun quickly and showed the results immediately, but I loved it.

I noticed counters inside the machine that the player could watch. These counters showed the denomination of the bills entered and the number of spins each reel made. With each spin the bill counters would add one, and the spin counter would change color. I wondered if that meant something. I found out later it did.

Late that afternoon I was playing the giant 10X machine. Around me people were standing in the lines waiting to check into the hotel. My favorite machine trudged along, one reel at a time. It would take about 10 seconds for all three reels to click to a stop in succession. I was watching the counters at the same time. For the first time, I noticed all of the counters were the same color and four of the counters were registering the same number, except for one. The fifth one was one number off. I made one pull more on the handle, and the reels spun again. On the reels I saw a red 7 come down, then a 10, and then a second 10. The lights were flashing and music was playing, that sweet flush of success came over me. I glanced down at the counters. Now the counters were all the same. It confirmed to me my theory was correct.

Several people who had heard the music were drawn to the machine. They gathered around me, offering me their congratulations. A guy dressed in a light blue tee-shirt and a pair of jeans rubbed my head, saying "I hope your luck rubs off on me." Another asked to rub my feet. I let them even though I thought it was a silly thing to do. A Japanese couple started snapping pictures of me and the machine. When they had finished, they each offered the word, "Omedetou" which I figured out to be congratulations, only in Japanese.

Apparently Mike had seen the commotion in the lobby and suspected I was in the middle of it. I saw him approaching me with a big smile on his face. He was amazed by the behavior of people in the lobby. He stood in awe as they gathered around me. I was the center of attention, and all I did was what came natural to me.

"I see it's happening again." He said, looked at me and the machine, and placed his hand on my shoulder as if he was standing guard over me. One of the well-wishers leaned over and said to him, "Stick close to her." He nodded as if to say, don't worry I will.

The slot attendant that came to pay the jackpot and took a photo of me winning yet another $10,000. I seemed to win lots of jackpots from slot machines that had 10 x symbols. viii After that experience, when I was out on the casino floor I had people bringing me drinks just so they could be near me while I played the machines. Maybe they thought they could pick up some tips by watching me play the machines. People visiting Las Vegas from other parts of the country and some from other parts of the world wanted to hang around with me. I didn't fight it; just gave into the whole Vegas scene. I had drawn attention to myself in a big way. People noticed someone that won huge amounts of money in a short amount of time. Certainly the casino did.

I was assigned a host to cater to my every whim. His name was Tony. Tony was a man in his early sixties with gray hair parted over to one side. His impeccable taste showed in everything he did. He dressed in an expensive three piece suit and everything he wore coordinated perfectly in color right down to his shoes and socks. As Tony introduced himself to me I detected what I thought was a New York accent in his voice.

"Are you from the East coast?"

"Yes I am. Born and raised in Brooklyn, New York." He said proudly, and added "I moved to Vegas when I was in my early twenties. I've been working at the Las Vegas Hilton before it was called that. In the old days, it was known as the International Hotel."

Tony immediately took Mike and me under his wing acting as if he needed to protect us from the glitz and corruption of the Vegas scene. Seemingly he was unaffected by it, or he had been there long enough to develop an immunity to it. Vegas had a reputation for chewing people up and spitting out the remains. The current ran fast. If you weren't a good swimmer, you drowned.

"My wife and I," Tony announced, "have been happily married for over forty years."

I supposed all marriages were subject to the same stresses and strains. With a city full of temptations like strippers, showgirls, and call girls, it was easy for men to stray. Tony was seemingly untouched by it all. He was comfortable with who he was, and happy with what he had. Not everyone could say that. Tony was the exception to the rule.

Tony attributed his blessings in life to his faith. He told us of his daily visits to the Catholic Church. Anyone who claimed his hero was Pope John Paul II was a person who took great pride in his faith. Never having been brought up with any religious background, I listened, but it was nothing that impressed me. I could respect people like Tony for being able to live their life on faith alone. I knew I could not live that way though.

I cannot say enough kind words that would describe my host Tony. He upgraded our room to a suite after his first meeting with us and extended our stay. Fresh flowers, a bottle of champagne, and chocolates were delivered daily along with a note from Tony. In his daily notes to me he would suggest his desire to make our stay in Las Vegas as well as at the hotel extraordinary. In his first note he asked my permission to allow him to make reservations to Las Vegas' finest eating establishments, all compliments of Tony. I trusted his judgment and allowed him to do what he did best, be the best host anyone could ever hope to have. Tony showered me and Mike with gifts while giving us advice on life and living at the start of each new day.

One of the sightseeing excursions Tony planned for us was a bus trip to the Hoover Dam. According to Tony it was a must-see for all travelers to Las Vegas, and as he said "I would be remiss in my duty if I didn't book it for you."

Early one morning we hopped on a tour bus that was parked outside the east wing of the hotel. When we stepped out into the open air I noticed the heat was rising off the pavement. It was only 10 am but the temperature was already 90 degrees so getting on the air-conditioned bus was a welcome relief.

About 30 minutes out from Vegas on the way to the Dam which was on the Arizona border we passed through a small town. It featured a post office and general store with some shacks sprinkled around it on both sides of the road. They were shaped like the Quonset huts the US Army built to house the troops during WWII. Over the intercom, the driver announced, "We are passing through Boulder City. This was the town that grew up around the dam to house the workers who built it. Look fast—what you see here is pretty much all that there is to the town."

After we passed through Boulder City, the desert lay out before us. On both sides of the road were rocky shelves that rose up from the desert as the bus drove through a winding canyon. The driver spoke up again, "If you look up on the rocks, you may catch a glimpse of the native goats that sit on the rocks." I didn't see anything, but a woman on the other side of the bus started yelling, "I see two over there", pointing out the window. I thought I caught a glimpse of a grey woolly hoofed shape off in the distance. Then it was out of sight as the bus moved onward around the next corner.

When we arrived at the dam a guide was waiting at the curb. He was a pleasant looking fellow dressed in a white shirt, tie, black pants, and wearing a construction helmet. After the bus was unloaded we formed a line and followed him. The first stop on the tour was at a memorial built on the road to commemorate the 96 workers who died while the dam was being constructed. Nearby on a bronze plaque an inscription proclaimed, "They died to make the desert bloom." Mike stepped to the edge and peered over the edge of the cliff.

"Be careful sir, it's a long way down to the spillway," the tour guide cautioned as he moved toward Mike. "96 workers died while the dam was under construction, we don't want to add to that."

"That's got to be a 1000 feet down." Mike noted as he backed up and got back in line.

"You could fit an Empire State building in the spillway, and you'd just about reach the top of the dam," the tour guide replied.

There was a buzz in the crowd hearing those facts and figures. We left the sign and walked down several flights of steps onto a platform next to the road. A museum, mechanical building, snack bar and administration building stood in a row.

"We are going to go into the mechanical building and down to the generation plant and I'll quickly show you the generators. Stay together, please."

We went through a side door and piled into an elevator. It took us down several floors. When we got off we wound through a passageway cut into the mountain. We passed through a double door that swung inward onto a platform. It looked out onto a room of rows of generators fixed to the concrete floor below. It seemed as long as a football field.

"These are the generators that power Las Vegas and the towns in the Valley of the Sun. The electricity is generated from the flow of the water into the dam from Lake Mead. The excess is run off down the spillway."

The tour guide started to rattle off facts and figures about the generation station but I was distracted by the loud hum that came from the generators. I could barely hear what he was saying. I looked at Mike and he was listening intently to what the tour guide was saying. When the tour guide was finished, he motioned toward the swinging doors. We retraced our steps to the elevators, and came back out onto the platform outside.

On the Nevada side of the dam stood two thirty foot tall bronze statues in front of a 200 foot cliff. They looked aged being exposed to the weather. The statues

Debbie Tosun Kilday

were perched on six foot tall platforms of shiny black and grey flecked stone flanked by a 142 foot flagpole. In front of the array a terrazzo star map was etched into the base depicting the celestial alignment on that site on the evening of September 30, 1935. That was the day President Franklin D. Roosevelt dedicated what was then called Boulder Dam.

The statues towered over us as the tour group gathered in front of them. The tour guide pointed at them and said "These statues are called the angels of the dam. They represent that eternal vigilance which is the price of liberty. People visiting Las Vegas generally come here to see the statues. According to the folklore, it is believed that if you rub the feet of the angels they will bring you good luck at the casinos. The feet of the statues have been rubbed by so many people, that the feet have become shiny."

Mike and I looked at each other. "It can't hurt to rub the feet, although I'm doing pretty well already." Mike nodded in agreement with me. Then we stood in line as one person after another walked up a few steps to the feet of the angels. Some people rubbed the feet vigorously. Others gently caressed them. When it came to be my turn, I looked up at the feet. The place where people were rubbing was shiny. It seemed like the tarnish which covered the rest of the statue had been rubbed off. I rubbed the feet and stepped back down. ix

The tour guide smiled. "For the remainder of the tour you can visit the dam, the snack bar, the museum or gift shop. Your bus will be leaving in one hour to return to Vegas." With that he waved goodbye, and headed off toward the museum. After we were done exploring the topside of the dam, we boarded the bus and headed back to Las Vegas.

Our limo driver Mary was more than happy to drive us anywhere we wanted to go in Vegas. All it took was a call to request a ride. We took advantage of that opportunity to see the sights and other casinos on the strip. The next evening I started partying at around 11:00pm in the fanciest and most expensive nightclubs on the strip. At the Bellagio it was the Petrossian Lounge and Caramel. At the Venetian it was Canaletto and Tao. At Caesar's it was Shadow Bar. At the Mirage it was Jet and Japonais Lounge. By 4:00am I was back to the slot machines at the Las Vegas Hilton to get down to the business of winning more money.

While making the rounds from one nightclub to the next I had my own entourage of admirers following me. I paid for all their drinks, show tickets, and meals. I spent money like it was going out of style. I was very confident I could always win more so I wasn't concerned at all. In Las Vegas you could potentially win more money than any other location in the world. The machines were primed to win. I think the machines were programmed to win more often, mainly because of the fierce competition amongst the different casinos. There were so many that each one had to try to draw people in by offering more than their competitors did.

In the original 4 day 3 night stay in Las Vegas which Tony had extended to 7 days by putting us in a suite, I had won over six figures playing dollar slot machines. Undercover agents working for the casino were watching me very closely trying to figure out if I was hiding some type of device on my person and were perplexed when they found out I wasn't cheating. They determined I was just 'lucky'. I didn't consider myself lucky, just very knowledgeable of the slot machines and how they worked and played.

When I mentioned this ability to other players they either called me 'Rain Man', the character that Dustin Hoffman played in the movie by the same name, or 'Lucky Lady'. They also wanted me to explain step by step what to do so they too could win. I was advised by a few people who observed my winning ways to write a book so they could buy it.

At every machine I sat at, people stopped to talk to me. After a while, they wanted to know what my secret to winning was. Besides my ability to look at a slot machine and be able to recognize where the machine was at in its programming, I did know one thing about myself that people may not know about me. With all I had seen and all I had been through in my life I sometimes thought that I should be hiding under a rock for cover to protect myself. Instead I said 'Yes', put myself out there, and opened myself up to new experiences even if it was painful at times. I always reminded myself of Kathy's words. *"Do not be afraid to be able."*

Whatever I was capable of I was grateful for the opportunity thus not wasting one second to experience it. My reasoning was: *Life is really short, for some shorter than others.* I no longer wanted to waste my time waiting for the right moment or the most comfortable situation. I put myself out there now, said "Yes" to new possibilities and I was not afraid like I used to be in my earlier years.

If someone were to ask me to describe myself today I would say, *I am not afraid to live, to love and to give to others that may be in need at this very moment in time.* If I recognized one thing it was the fact that all of us were connected so we should not judge others by their actions as long as they did not willfully hurt anyone else.

In Las Vegas they didn't do anything on a small scale. They were not timid or frugal. The casino personal did whatever it took to make you feel comfortable and happy while visiting there. Mike and I were treated by my new host Tony like we were royalty. I was sent to get a complete makeover Vegas style at the spa in the Las Vegas Hilton. I was given a personal assistant by my host Tony to dress me, give me a new hairdo, and jewelry. This included a complete wardrobe for that evening for Mike and I. Tony put it all on the Hilton's tab. All this was in preparation to see Barry Manilow in concert. I had always admired Barry and his music and couldn't wait to see him in person.

After the show we would be introduced to him and go to an afterhours catered get together. We were seated in the first row stage left. All I could say about Barry Manilow was that he was a real professional and never disappointed. His music was timeless and his lyrics were heartfelt. In my opinion his show was a breathtaking spectacle of music, voice, and dance. The show was so well choreographed and the visual effects were so outstanding that it was something that will stay in our hearts forever. We thoroughly enjoyed every minute of the concert and looked forward to meeting him after the show.

While walking down the stairs to Barry's dressing room, we didn't know what to expect. Some celebrities became egomaniacs once they reached the top of their profession. This was not the case at all with Barry. He was tired after the show but that didn't stop him from coming right over and introducing himself to us. He asked us our names and wanted to know where we were from. When he found out we were also from the East Coast he seemed excited. We talked with him like he was a friend rather than a celebrity and met all the other members of his band. He treated them as if they were a part of his family, and they responded in kind.

Because I felt comfortable with him, I asked, "Could you do me a favor Barry?"

Hearing the request, a smile crept across his suntanned face. I supposed he was getting requests from fans all of the time.

"Could you call my girlfriend Patsy and just say 'hi' to her? She's a huge fan of yours." I realized it was about 2 am on the East Coast and I knew she would be in bed.

Barry didn't hesitate at all and thought it would be fun to hear her reaction. "I'll do my best. Put her on the line."

As I took out my cell phone, Barry said, "Why don't you dial it for me?"

It rang several times before she answered. Then she answered like it had awakened her. I handed the cell phone to Barry.

Barry said, "Hi Patsy, its Barry. How are you, I hope I didn't wake you up."

I imagined her lying in bed trying to figure out who Barry was and why he would call at this early morning hour. Everyone in that room could hear Patsy's scream over my cell phone when she recognized who she was talking to. She was so happy and didn't mind at all that Barry Manilow had awakened her from her sleep.

Barry got a kick out of it and said to me, "I guess I still got it."

We all laughed. I couldn't tell you how impressed I was with Barry. He donated so much of his time and money to give to others in need. He was a special person in more ways than one, and he was so nice. He told us he would look forward to seeing us again either in Las Vegas or on the East coast. As it turned out we would see him several more times in concert and were always invited to the afterhour's gatherings he planned for friends. A photo was taken of Mike and I with Barry Manilow as a memento of the occasion.

The few days we spent in Las Vegas were memorable. I was given every gift they offered in the gift shop at the Las Vegas Hilton. I thoroughly enjoyed every minute spent there. My only problem was I had slept very little during the time we spent there. Even as a teenager I had never required much sleep. My mind was always active and analyzing everything. While in Las Vegas I didn't feel I could rest or sleep for fear I would miss out on something. Since Kathy's death I had changed the whole way I viewed and ran my life.

My experience with Kathy and Jon's untimely deaths had taught me something. It was that: *Most people take things for granted thinking that there is always another day, another chance. Tomorrow may not come for some of us so you had better live today as if it is your last day. If you care for someone, don't wait to tell them or show them. If you need to tell someone something important tell them now, not later. If you live your life in this manner you will find that you live in this moment in time and realize you do anyway whether you realize it or not. Just let go of your fear and enjoy life.*

The night before we were to leave Las Vegas, I wanted to stay at the Hilton instead of exploring other casinos. After dinner I sat down to play a three coin dollar slot machine with a bunch of sevens. Out of the corner of my eye I saw some stairs going down into a room with just a few slot machines in it. I walked down the stairs to investigate.

Once I was downstairs I noticed that the sounds of the casino were gone, replaced by near silence. It was a small room filled with slot machines. Most of them were very high-denominations like $100 and $500. On the walls were portraits of Elvis and pictures of him in concert. A man wearing a casino attendant uniform had been standing in the corner. He approached me.

"Are you lost?"

"I'm not lost, just curious what this room is."

"It's the high roller lounge. There are two rooms actually." He pointed to a door in one of the corners of the room behind a slot machine.

"Why is it so quiet in here?"

"Both rooms are heavily soundproofed."

"Why?"

"Because these rooms were once Elvis's personal hideaway when he wasn't performing... Do you want to play any of the machines?"

I said "Sure, I'll give them a try."

"They only take special $100 tokens." When I heard that I almost said never mind and left. One hundred dollar machines were a little out of my league. But I figured what the hell. I opened my purse and took out five one hundred dollar bills and gave them to the

116

attendant. In exchange he gave me five tokens. All of the machines took only one token per spin.

I started to play one of the black and white machines. On my first spin I won a thousand dollars. All the while I was wondering why I was the only person in this room playing these machines. Then suddenly a hostess walked through the doorway of the other room and motioned to me to come over when she saw me.

"Would you like to join the other high rollers in the next room for a bite to eat?" I had just started playing the Black and White machine and was hesitant to leave it when it had money in it.

The slot attendant intervened. "You could come back to get paid for your win any time. Don't worry about walking away from the machine."

As I walked through the doorway I was astonished to see about twelve people eating finger foods and drinking drinks. The two rooms were so soundproofed that I had been totally unaware that others were in the room next to where I had been. Some were standing and some were sitting. I noticed several plush over-stuffed chairs and some tables against the walls. I went over to the buffet of food items on one of the tables to take a look. I took a plate and put a few pieces of celery and carrots to munch on. I saw a wooden chair that looked like an antique. It had two curved arms and a blue velvet cushion. No one was sitting on it so I decided to sit down to rest while eating.

The hostess came over to me. "Are you comfortable?"

I said, "Yes, very."

"That was Elvis's chair. He always sat in it while resting in this room. He liked it very much too."

Emotions took over me and tears welled up in my eyes. I was sitting in the King of Rock and Roll's chair. I imagined Elvis trying to get away from the crowds and noise and just sitting and resting in that chair long ago just as I was doing now. After eating my snack I thanked the hostess and the attendant. I went back into the other room to gather my winnings and then headed upstairs to our room. Mike had already gone up before me and was in bed almost asleep. I woke him gently to tell him of my little adventure. I felt sad while telling the story feeling sorry for Elvis and myself. I related to him wanting to hide away from the crowds of people and the noise if just for a little while. I fell asleep almost immediately after getting undressed and getting into bed. The morning seemed to come quickly.

Upon checkout my host Tony personally came to say goodbye to me. It was his day off but he made a special trip to say goodbye to me. I felt so honored and thought his actions were so kind. I had bought him some designer ties as a gift for all his kindness towards me. I would have left them behind with a thank you note on his desk. I was glad I could give them to him in person. He looked so happy it made my day. He gave me a big hug and a kiss, put us in Mary's limo and we headed off to McCarran Airport to go home to Connecticut.

12 – Don't Look Back, You Can Never Look Back

Once at the airport before checking in, I decided to play one of the slot machines they had in the aisles there. I picked a Black Gold dollar machine. On my first twenty dollars I won $1,250. The employees at the airport were not used to seeing anyone win anything on the airport machines. It took them forty minutes to process the W2G ticket because they first had to scramble to find a blank form. I laughed at their incompetence but still gave them a fair tip.

Before returning home from Las Vegas I had to buy an extra suitcase to hold all the stuff we had acquired from the casinos while in Las Vegas. Here I found myself at McCarran Airport holding a carry on suitcase filled with $375,000 standing in line at airport security. I could have gone to the bank while there or converted it to a check but I found it lots more fun to just take the cash. As soon as my suitcase was x-rayed, a swarm of federal agents surrounded me, separated me from Mike and they cleared the area of other passengers. I was taken to a room nearby by federal agents. I felt manhandled as they took me by the forearms and one of the female agents nails dug into my skin. I was questioned for more than an hour. I had to show each W2G slip and explain what had happened to the other money I had won. After all the questioning I was finally let go. I was angry and felt raped by the system and generally abused by people.

With my ten years of martial arts training in my younger years I wanted to go against all my training and kick everyone's ass. Instead here I was years later, the most patient, the most quiet and passive looking person to others looking at me from the outside. Inside there was a different story to tell. I was always on the edge, acutely aware and not always liking it. Getting settled into my seat on the airplane, I fell asleep for most of our flight going home. I was exhausted from the ordeal I had to endure at airport security.

As our plane started to descend onto the runway at Bradley Memorial Airport, instead of going straight home from the airport I wanted to go to Mohegan Sun. *I must be a true 'degenerate' gambler to make a crazy statement like that. This might sound odd to anyone reading this but it also sounds odd to me.* I felt like I had to check in at my casino home before returning to my real home. It had only been a week since I had gone to Las Vegas although it seemed like an eternity. Mike agreed to go to the casino but told me he didn't want to stay long there and I agreed.

As soon as we got to the Riverview Garage and parked the car, I went inside the Sky Casino and headed to and sat down at the original machine that started it all for me. Mike went off in another direction to play his favorite quarter machines. The row where I was sitting was empty this time being it was 4:00am. I looked up at the explanation of possible wins and looking at the $10,000 win I knew I needed to affirm my ability to win just by my sheer desire and determination alone. I put a hundred dollar bill into the machine and turned away from the machine so that I could not see the possible programming clues. Why was I doing this? I was challenging myself once again.

Perhaps also it was because of my thoughts of my parents always thinking I wasn't good enough. No matter what accomplishments I had in my life I was never given any credit or even a pat on the back for a job well done. *Being treated poorly by loved ones screws around with your head.* After a few spins I had won three hundred dollars. I turned to look quickly and then turned away from the machine again. As I kept playing the machine I realized something I had never realized before that night. Not only could I see the possible programming of the machine as the wheels in my mind turned as well as in the machine, but I could also 'hear' the clues while playing. When I would hit a cherry I could hear a little sound telling me that. I knew without having to look at the machine that by the number of cherry's I had hit and the time in-between each one that my machine was heading for the top jackpot. I kept playing and then knew I must be near the end of my money now. I turned and looked to see how many coins I had left in the machine. I was down to nine coins or three more spins. Now I turned back towards my machine and looking at it I hit the button. Nothing came up. I had two more spins and that would be it. I wasn't going to put in another hundred dollar bill I had decided. I hit the button again and it happened fast but I saw it in my mind a split second before I saw it on the face of the machine. The ten times symbol, the ten times symbol, the red seven. I had won the ten thousand dollars jackpot yet again.

I asked a girl that was just walking by to take a photo of me next to my latest $10,000 win. In exchange for taking the photo I gave her a thousand dollars for her trouble. I was feeling generous as usual. *You can't make lots of money unless you are willing to give away money as well. The motto is, Give and you shall receive.*[x]

After the attendant came to take my tax info and then came back with my money I called Mike on his cell phone and told him I was ready to go home now. I decided I wouldn't tell anyone this story of that night until now because I wasn't sure anyone would believe it and felt it would just be considered as bragging and I didn't want that. The next day I called Nellie to see how she was doing. Nellie filled me in. While we were in Vegas, things hadn't been going well at home.

"Deb, I am doing okay but John's Mom died two days ago. I didn't want to ruin your time in Vegas knowing you and Mike would be home soon enough. I have been helping John with the funeral arrangements. His sister Kim will be here tomorrow. He had a few drinks last night which is understandable. I didn't say anything and tried to ignore it given the circumstances. I am afraid for him Deb. I don't know if I can be with him if he starts drinking like he used to when we first met."

Mike and I attended John's Mom's funeral and tried to give our support to him and his sister. Afterwards John invited us to his house saying that he didn't want to be alone. At the house John immediately poured two drinks and while holding out both arms holding the two drinks in each hand he gave a toast.

"One for me and one for you, Mom, wherever you are."

He downed one drink and then the other. As soon as he had drunk them, he was filling both glasses up for another round. His sister Kim thanked us for coming and told John she was tired and went to bed. The night progressed with Nellie looking on at John like a scared little girl while he poured two drinks at a time and drank them both, one after another. I was feeling like I needed a few drinks myself and wanted to be a friend to John at the same time. It had been a long time since I had a drink of hard liquor, but I now found myself drinking and toasting as John drowned himself in good quality Irish whiskey. I was feeling no pain by the fifth, sixth or was it the seventh or eighth shot? I knew I was not in control of my faculties but I didn't care.

Sometimes you just had to be reckless and let go of all your inhibitions. This seemed like as good a time as any. At first Mike and Nellie didn't want to participate but after awhile they too started to appreciate the taste of good quality Irish whiskey. Even though I was stinking drunk I still had to be the level-headed dope and think that there was no one to drive us all home. I hated always being the thinker, caregiver, the one that made sure everyone else was safe from harm. As it turned out it didn't matter because we all either passed out or fell asleep on the couch.

The next morning I was the second one to awaken. John was the first. I got up off of the couch and walked over to John. Putting my arms around his neck and with my forehead against his, I gave him a hug and a kiss saying, "Move ahead with your life. Your mom wouldn't want you to wallow in sadness."

He responded with, "I think I needed to hear that— Thanks for being my friend."

Debbie Tosun Kilday

I took charge of his kitchen and started to prepare breakfast as all the others started to awaken from their drunken sleep. I felt like John was the brother I never had and wished I had family like him in my life. Actually he was my family even though we were not born into it and had to wait fifty plus years before meeting.

A couple of weeks later Mike left to go on a business trip to Texas for two weeks. I didn't want to be home alone so I decided to spend most of my time at the casino. I called up my host and asked for a hotel room for the two weeks. I had heard that Stevie Wonder would be playing in the Arena so I asked for one ticket to see him. I had asked Nellie if she would go to the concert with me but she was busy with John and I understood that.

When arriving at Mohegan Sun to check into my room I wasn't expecting anything special. The rooms were always clean and very comfortable. I never was in my room most of the time while staying there so I didn't feel like I needed a fancy room, just a place to rest or sleep for a few hours. The woman checking me into my room at the hotel desk started to check me in. Midway through her typing, she stopped and told me to wait for a few minutes. She left the desk and went into the back room for about three minutes. I wondered what the holdup was but stood there patiently.

"Thank for your patience." Then she handed me my room key.

"Since you will be with us for two weeks, we gave you a room with an excellent view."

I responded with, "Thank you."

I collected my room keys and headed towards the elevators. After getting past the attendant by showing

124

him my room key, I looked at the key myself before getting on the elevator so that I would know what floor to get off. Usually I would ask for a room on the lower levels near the elevators as my preference, being I was mostly downstairs in the Sky Casino. Looking at the key I noticed I was either on the top floor of the hotel or close to it.

After getting off of the elevators I looked at the signs to find out what direction to head towards to get to my room. Looking at the signs my room was at the end of the hall overlooking the Thames River. It took me awhile to walk down the long corridor to where my room was.

Upon opening the door I gasped at the sight in front of me. My room was the size of a quarter of that whole floor. Every room had large picture windows overlooking the river view. I had two bedrooms, one master bedroom and one guest. Each had its own bath and walk in closet. All the bathrooms had a shower stall plus bathtubs with a window so that you could gaze out at the river while bathing. I had a full kitchen, dining room, living room, den and even an office fully equipped. Each room including the baths had a television and stereo system in them.

I found myself in this room made for royalty yet I was by myself with no one to share this experience with. I always carried a small Nikon digital camera in my purse in case I needed to take a photo and didn't have my full size digital camera with me. I took out my camera and started to photograph each room so that I could have proof of my stay in this gorgeous room. I couldn't believe this was my room and didn't expect anyone else to believe I had been given a room like this for my two week stay.

Debbie Tosun Kilday

I took full advantage of my room which was the size of a small house. I called down to the front desk and asked if I could have some groceries brought up so that I didn't have to always eat out. My every desire was fulfilled by the staff. I was even offered a private chef if I so desired but I declined. The night before the Stevie Wonder concert I had been playing the slot machines until eleven that night before retiring to my room. I was so enjoying my room that I couldn't wait to get back to it and relax by watching a movie or just sitting on the sofa reading a book. It was around midnight when I started to hear someone singing and playing the piano. I figured out quickly that Stevie Wonder was in the suite next to mine. I listened carefully to the song coming from Stevie's room. It sounded like he was singing "My Cherie Amor". I was being serenaded by Stevie Wonder without him knowing it.

The next night I went to see him in concert. I had been given a seat in the second row. I love his music and his voice. His concert was so special both for the musical experience plus knowing I was in the presence of a musical legend. I enjoyed the whole experience of the two weeks. At first I was hesitant to be by myself. During my stay I realized I needed that time alone. The two weeks were truly a relaxing and rejuvenating experience for me that I will never forget.

On average Mike and I were going to two concerts a week. Most of the time we would invite others to join us. It was hard to keep track of what day it was. Every day was like a party for others but for me it was just another work day. I did enjoy myself but it was also taxing on me at times.

To let you know just how devoted I was to playing slots, a few weeks after Stevie Wonder came to Mohegan Sun, I almost missed a concert with The Who. I was so focused on playing a Blazing Sevens machine because it was close to winning the progressive jackpot of twelve hundred dollars. After winning that jackpot I began playing another Blazing Sevens machine knowing I could win several hundred dollars more. I lost track of the time as I continued to win several jackpots. Eventually I looked at the time and rushed over to the Arena. I made it to the Arena right before intermission. The Who was the second act on the bill. I had missed most of the opening act which was The Pretenders. They were one of my favorite bands. To this day, I still think about missing most of The Pretenders. But it was for a 'good cause'. If I didn't keep working hard to win jackpots, we would be missing all the rest of the concerts. It meant keeping my level of play high. In order to do that, I had to work hard at winning jackpots.

13 – Other forms of Hard Work

Most people think that if you did not get dirt on your hands and had sweat pouring off your brow, you did not do an honest day's or night's work. I had worked for years in numerous factories and even in the computer operations field using cancer causing chemicals, wearing oil soaked clothes, breathing in the fumes of liquid plastic sealants, and what did I get for all that hard work? I will tell you what I got. I got asthma, cancer, and $3.60 an hour.

No one ever complained or thought badly about how I made a living back then. Now to supplement my disability checks, I walked into a casino, sat down at a slot machine, started with a hundred dollar bill and made on average $500 an hour. This way of supplementing my income was totally unacceptable to all of my family and most of my friends. I was told repeatedly that I better get help to stop going there or I would be disowned.

The line was: *No decent person would go to a casino as often as you do, and I don't want to associate with 'people like that.'* I wasn't bullied by that negative line of thinking and because I wasn't, I was discarded by most of my family and friends. Let me clarify that statement. I was ignored and forgotten until they heard that Elton John, Aerosmith, Billy Joel, The Who, Bon Jovi, Tony Bennett, Ringo Starr, Van Halen, Hall & Oates, Barry

Manilow, etc. were coming to play a concert at Mohegan Sun. Then I was temporarily treated very nicely with a big fat fake smile all in their quest to have me score complimentary concert tickets for them. While I was at it I could also get them a hotel room for the night and dinner arrangements at one of the high end restaurants. I could also book them a two hour massage at the spa.

I was golden one second and tarnished the next. I even had an uncle that disowned me and cut me out of his will after he asked me to answer one question for him. He asked if it was true that I frequented the casino and I answered yes. Since answering that question I haven't heard from him since. I tried to contact him several times but he wouldn't take any of my calls or acknowledge me at all. I guess that showed how much I meant to family. It made me realize that if I had been the type to be sensitive to this kind of treatment I would have maybe done myself in or listen to them and not go back to the casino. *I have been through too much to be that sensitive and I'll be damned if anyone is going to tell me what to do, how to live, who to love and who to hang out with.*

People thought it was easy to make the kind of money I was making at the casino. It wasn't to tell the truth. True, I made more money than most everyone I knew. It was probably the hardest work I had ever done in my life. I had to put in many hours of playing to accumulate the amounts of money I would walk out of there with. I had to figure out what machines to play, when to leave them if they stopped paying out, how to play them so they would continue to pay. My mind was constantly taxed while playing as I did my best to keep the money coming my way.

There were times when I just wanted to give in, give up and get out. It wasn't easy for me to see the greed shown me by people that used to say they loved me and now had no use for me unless I was giving them what they desired like more money or more material things. I had never felt so hurt. I was still hurting from that kind of jealousy and greed. I will never really get over it but instead I analyzed the situation and decided that I didn't need people like that in my life anymore no matter who they were.

There was an old song from the 1970's Rod Stewart recorded called "The first cut is the deepest". It was a song about your first love affair going bad, and how you felt because of it. The message of the song was *how do you try to love again?* The rejection I was feeling now was a little different. It was from cuts received when being used and abused by people who you thought loved you. They were piling on because they thought they could bully me into doing what they wanted me to do for them. By ganging up on me, they reasoned I would cave. They made it seem like they were doing it for my own good. When you were young and impressionable that worked. When you had been through the mill like I had, and survived it, that didn't work so well. I knew that scars healed, memories faded, and time marched on.

The pain and rejection I was feeling didn't linger for too long. I recognized that the freeloaders had their own agenda. They wanted something I could give them. It was something they couldn't get for themselves. That was a free ride on the 'gravy train'. It didn't matter to them that I had to work hard for it. The only thing that mattered to them was it was there for the taking if they could get their hands on it. Realizing that, I had to just let it go.

14 – The Crumbling Cookie

It had now been three whole years since my first visit to the casino. Each new year fifty to eighty dollars was being deducted from my disability check before my check was deposited into my checking account each month. Each year I was put into a higher tax bracket. Each year I was taxed on my winnings and on any losses I may have had as well. I was now being taxed at the highest percentage allowed by the U.S. federal government. Times were changing but not for the better. The economy was showing that it could not survive the Bush years.

One night while at the casino, I noticed that maintenance was being done on several banks of machines that I played often. One such machine was the dollar Blazing Sevens progressive jackpot machine. Another type of machine was the Quick Hit progressive dollar machines. Unable to play those machines that night, I didn't stay long before leaving and going back home. I had favorite machines and didn't like playing machines just for the sake of playing. I always played machines I knew would consistently win and keep winning.

The next night I decided I would go back to the casino by myself to play my favorite machines. I saw that the Blazing Seven's machines were back up and running. I put in a hundred dollar bill as I never put in anything less than a hundred dollar bill into a dollar machine. As I started playing the machine I immediately noticed something different with the machine. Usually when you would play one coin, the progressive jackpot would advance one penny, two coins, two pennies, three coins, three pennies. At that moment I realized that it was making no difference if I played one coin or three coins. The machine was only advancing one penny for three coins in.

I knew that now the programming had been changed the night before during the maintenance done by the casino personnel. I knew what these new changes meant too. It meant that now it would take three times longer and three times the amount of money to win the same progressive jackpot. In prior years the machines ran in one cycle. Now they were running in three cycles.

To say I was upset by these changes was an understatement. I continued to play my hundred dollar bill and began winning two and three hundred dollars every few spins. By the time I had played in half of the hundred dollars I had already exceeded the progressive jackpot amount. I was up by twelve hundred dollars. Knowing I would have no chance at winning the progressive jackpot for another two cycles or more, I cashed out my winnings and went over to my favorite machine in the casino, the Bally's Bonus Times 2x, 10x, 5x. I put a hundred dollar bill into the machine and started playing it. I noticed that these machines were now programmed differently too. What I was seeing on the face of the machine was much different than what I had seen in the past.

There is a term for this in casino language. It is the fact that the machines had been 'tightened'. To explain

Debbie Tosun Kilday

this in simple terms it means that there were less open spaces inside the machine or blanks to put it plainly. That means that the machine reels would spin several times more before landing on a payout.

My guess was these could be three times tighter or more. This was really taking out the fun of playing my favorite slot machines. I cashed out after losing close to twenty five hundred dollars, beaten down and depressed. I thought about leaving and not returning to the casino at that point. I had been going there too long to do that. I had become accustomed to the VIP status and wasn't the type to give up too easily.

As time went on, it got harder and harder to win big money. Even though I continued winning, the experience wasn't like the previous three years. Most of my casino friends were gone. Some had lost so much money they had to declare bankruptcy. Most were so unhappy with the way things had become, they gave up going to the casino altogether.

On one particular night I had four hundred dollars in free play. I figured I would go and try my luck using just the free play the casino had sent me. I would make up these small challenges for myself. I think boredom was the motivation. I walked towards the Pit. I could have played a five dollar machine but decided to go all the way. I walked over to the Wheel of Fortune hundred dollar machine. I have a self destructive streak at times when feeling depressed. This was one of those times.

I decided to play a hundred dollar Wheel of Fortune machine. Looking up at the payoff amounts given I got a spin, I could not win anything less than three thousand dollars if I got a spin. The question was would I get a spin or have to leave empty handed. I usually did not favor playing the Wheel of Fortune machines especially the dollar ones. They took too much money before landing on a spin. If you were to land on a spin you would have already lost way too much money to make your money back.

I punched in two hundred dollars into the machine to use my free play. I figured I would save the other two hundred for later. I spun the machine and got—nothing. I wondered at a hundred dollars a spin how this would turn out. I spun again. This time I got a two coin win which was equal to a cherry but in this case two hundred dollars. I was okay with the fact that this would buy me two more spins if nothing else. This could also mean that I was heading towards a spin. I spun the machine again and got—nothing. I spun the machine again and got a spin. I was absolutely elated at this outcome. I was happy this was casino money and not my own. I sat there with the machine beeping waiting for me to hit the button to spin the wheel. I hit the button and the wheel started to turn. It had already gone past the three thousand dollar mark so I started to get excited. It landed on fifteen thousand dollars. *Not bad*, I thought, *in fact great!*

Even though I was thinking this, I was not really acting like it was a big deal. *Am I really that numb to winning I can no longer appreciate it?* While waiting for the attendant to come I punched in another hundred into in the machine to my right which was not one of my favorite machines. It was a hundred dollar Double Diamond machine. I never really liked the diamond machines no matter if they were diamonds, double diamonds, etc. I spun the hundred dollar Double Diamond machine and a double diamond symbol landed on the first position. A second double diamond symbol landed in the second position. In the third position came three bars. I had to look twice to try to figure out what this meant. Three bars were six thousand dollars and two symbols were four times six thousand and being this was a hundred dollar machine I had just won twenty four thousand dollars. *Not bad for a nights work,* I thought to myself.

I didn't have any friends in this area of the casino. It was too rich for them. I sat there thinking about how hard all this was becoming and how much it really was not fun anymore. I was sitting alone with no one to share my good fortune with and feeling sorry for myself. *No one really cares,* I thought to myself.

All of a sudden someone was approaching me from my left. It wasn't the attendant. It was Taxman. I yelled out loud when I saw who it was, "Shit, what do you want now?"

He sat down next to me and put his arm around my neck leaning in towards me trying to kiss me and rub his arm against my breast. I quickly removed his prying hands off of me. He started to laugh at my disgust for him.

I said to him, "What is fucking wrong with you?"

His smiling face turned sour at that moment as he said to me, "You are going to have to pay me directly from now on if you don't want certain government officials to come knocking on your door."

I said. "Are you out of your fucking mind?

He leaned closer so no one else would overhear our conversation. "Well, I could take something else in exchange. It doesn't have to be in the form of cash."

I said, "Like what?" Perhaps I was a little naïve but I couldn't imagine what he was driving at with that remark.

When he saw the puzzled look on my face, he dropped the bomb. "I have always been interested in you and not only for your abilities at the slot machines even though that is a real turn on."

At that moment my favorite attendant Gus was approaching me. Gus must have noticed I was not looking like a happy camper. I should have been looking happy after winning fifteen thousand on one machine and twenty four thousand on the next.

Gus asked, "Are you okay Debbie?"

I figured I didn't need Gus involved in this obvious extortion attempt of sex, money, or both by Taxman.

I said to Gus, "I am fine Gus thanks for asking, but I need you to process my win so I can get the hell out of here and head home early."

As soon as I got paid I gave Gus a five thousand dollar tip. It was my obvious attempt to show Taxman I couldn't be controlled by him. I also wanted to show him that he wasn't going to get one damn dime from me. Taxman looked at me in surprise but he wasn't as surprised as Gus was. After Gus thanked me profusely and left the area, I was left with Taxman and me as the only two people in that whole area.

I said to Taxman, "You are not getting one damn dime from me you bastard."

Taxman smiled. He seemed to relish my defiant attitude like it might have turned him on. "So you have decided to take me up on my other offer?"

I said to Taxman, "No. Do what you have to do, whatever that is, but you aren't getting anything from me directly or indirectly."

"I am sorry to hear you say that Deb. We could have been good together. You are a very attractive woman with curves in all the right places. I was really looking forward to showing you a good time. Some women appreciate my abilities in the bedroom and crave more after I am done pleasuring them."

Somehow I did not think any woman would lust after Taxman for any reason whatsoever. I wanted to gag just envisioning it. I was really pissed that he thought he could act like he knew me personally and call me Deb.

Even though he could tell by my reaction I was repulsed by his advances, he persisted. "If you don't want to take a chance and let me show you what real ecstasy is, I will have to turn you over to the field office where you will have to suffer the consequences."

I wasn't sure what he meant by that but I felt I had to ask him a question. I turned to him and said, "Why me? Why pick on me? I never hurt anyone. All I ever did was try to help other people."

Taxman smiled again and said, "When you went to Las Vegas and came back saying you had won $630,000 and paid $240,000 tax, certain government officials surmised you must have won much more than that. They are thinking in the amount of $980,000 to be exact. They don't like anyone trying to get away with not paying them and want the money they think you owe them. I have been watching you because frankly it is amazing to watch you turn a hundred dollar bill into thousands and thousands, and you aren't even cheating. I have never seen anyone like you in my years as an investigator. You also have a nice ass. You can't blame a guy for trying."

I turned to Taxman with a smirk on my face. "Thanks for the compliments even though you are one crude bastard." I even surprised myself with that remark. "Before I leave to go home do you want to go have a drink with me in the lounge?"

Taxman looked very pleased with himself like he was making headway as he answered, "Yes."

After all this truth telling I wasn't really mad at him. I took him into the lounge and had a conversation with him. As the saying goes, *Keep your friends close, but keep your enemies closer.*

We talked about his job, how long he had been working there, how he traveled to different locations to investigate people that try to lie and cheat their way out of paying their taxes. As far as his tactics were concerned, I had to know just how successful they were. I found it hard to believe he hadn't been brought up on charges of sexual harassment.

"How much more do you make extorting money from people or bullying them into having sex with you?"

He didn't act apologetic or remorseful when he said casually, "Quite a bit more Deb, as a matter of fact."

At the end of our conversation we both knew where we stood. Now that I understood Taxman a little better I wasn't as intimidated by him as I was before. Thinking back maybe I should have slept with him even though knowing myself, I never would have even considered doing anything like that. I will tell you this though. It would have been a lot easier than what lay ahead for me; What a night, what a life!

Before leaving the casino that night I contacted a casino friend of mine by the name of Matt. I had met Matt in the Sachem Lounge through my friend Mark. I usually didn't see Matt in other locations in the casino because we played different games. He exclusively played video poker which I did not. Matt worked for the State as a tax auditor.

He was very good at playing video poker but not as good as I was playing slots. I had to admit that playing video poker took a lot more skill than playing slots. His expertise was his vast knowledge in all areas of taxing and even Nellie would consult him with tough tax questions she might have had at times. I called Matt on his cell phone and left him a message to call me back. He always screened all his calls before calling people back. It was just a habit of his. He called me back in less than three minutes after I had called him and left him a message. I returned the call and we made arrangements to meet in the Sachem Lounge.

When Matt walked into the lounge he walked to the bar before coming to meet me. Matt was a big drinker of all drinks containing vodka. I can't remember a time when he did not have a drink in his hand. Matt was a man in his early fifties, quite good looking with light brown hair and dark brown eyes. Matt got his drink and sat down with me at a small table in the corner of the lounge. I had chosen that table because it was out of the way. I didn't want anyone else listening in on our conversation.

After I told Matt about Taxman's visit with me, a look of genuine concern came over his face. Matt liked to joke around. Generally he was a happy-go-lucky guy who liked to play practical jokes on people. His demeanor had changed as if he had just dropped a bundle on a video poker machine.

"Deb, I have heard a story similar to yours from only two other people in my whole career. Shit, you are in real trouble if someone like that is monitoring you. People like that are no good Deb. The people that send them to watch you are even worse. You are screwed is all I can say. It would be great if I could say you will be okay but I won't lie to you. These people are bloodsuckers and will drain you of any extra money they think you might have until there is nothing left. Usually they pick on people that already have money not someone like you. I find it unusual that they are picking on you. I would help you if I could but someone like me at the state level is no match for those guys." His voice had a serious tone I wasn't used to hearing from him.

Matt got up from the table and as he bent down to give me a hug said, "I wish you luck my friend because you are going to need it."

He got away from me as soon as he could like I was radioactive. At that moment I knew I was in real trouble. After Matt left, I sat there for a moment to let Matt's reaction soak in. Matt was a tax accountant who had considerable experience in these matters, and he was showing genuine concern. It gave me pause to think of the seriousness of my situation. What could I do? I didn't have a clue. I knew I wasn't going to solve it right then so I decided to head home myself.

While driving the long drive home I worried what would happen to me. I also didn't want Mike involved in this. He didn't need this kind of hassle. Neither did I but I was used to bad treatment already. This all started out with me just trying to help Kathy pay for her cancer treatments. That seemed like a lifetime ago now.

During the next week I got a letter in the mail from a certain government agency asking me to come into their local office in two weeks. I was to bring all my W2G slips from all the years up to this point and also to bring proof of my play at each and every casino I had ever stepped foot in. I would have to write a script for the last three years telling them all the dates and times and what machines I played and how much money I played into each machine. I also had to tell them how much money I went in with, came home with, and how much money I had given away to others. I had my work cut out for me.

The abuse I had endured from family seemed like a birthday party compared to this. At that moment I felt utterly and totally alone. Normally I wouldn't burden anyone I cared for with what was happening to me. I wasn't the whining type. I created this situation and I would now face the music alone. The next day I went and bought a blank journal at Barnes and Noble Bookstore. I started to write out my history in preparation of my upcoming visit to the 'Agency'.

In the next two weeks before my visit with them I stayed up all night, every night after Mike went to bed. I was writing my script in secret. The stress took its toll on my health. I knew I now had an ulcer because I saw the signs by the bleeding. I ignored the signs of my failing health. I certainly did not go to the casino during this time either. I guess the one thing I could say that was a positive in this situation was that I was a survivor and I would never, ever give up. Only time would tell if I could survive this.

My son always tells me *"Mom, you are the strongest person I know."* I didn't feel very strong at that moment. More importantly I didn't want to be strong. I wished I could allow myself to be weak but that was not an option for me. There had never been anyone in my life that I could turn to or lean on. It may be sad to say, but not one other person ever wanted to do something for me without wanting something in return. Everyone needed to feel the warmth of a hug, a tender kiss on the cheek or even a sympathetic ear. I had always given that to everyone I knew but I had never felt that in return. Others always depended on me to be the responsible one that took care of them.

At times I would justify my actions by thinking that others didn't have to feel the pain of utter loneliness as I did. In my mind I would convince myself that if I endured and sacrificed myself, someone else might be spared. I would always be there for them and they counted on that. They could count on me as I never faltered as a caregiver. I would not want anyone to feel the despair I have felt. That kind of utter loneliness created stress that left me empty and hollow inside. At times I have wished I could remake myself into one of the many heartless bastards just looking out for number one. That was someone that would throw anyone else under the bus just to save themselves.

The sad truth is: I can't change myself because I don't want to. I am too passionate and caring for my own good. The only person I can blame for that is myself. People might assume that because I am competent I don't need anyone to hold my hand or guide me. Even a strong person like me needs that at least once in their life; just to know someone cared before they die. Not having it

Debbie Tosun Kilday

makes you feel like you're not worthy of life. I am sure others have taken their own life over lesser things. I had to convince myself to fight and not become one of the many statistics.

15 – I Can See Clearly Now

Since I am a very methodical person, I handle things in increments. First I had to get my house in order for the inquisition I was facing. As I organized all my W2G slips according to date, time and year, I put them inside a folder I had bought at Staples. In my journal I started to write my casino history remembering the day by day activities. At the same time I paused and thought about the detailed events of some of the particular days as well.

I thought of all the concerts I had attended as I looked over the hundreds of concert ticket stubs I had in my possession. Each concert held special memories of the different performers I had seen through the years. There was one in particular I relished above all. I will never forget the thrill I felt in my heart after meeting Ringo for the first time.

The Beatles are my favorite band of all time but meeting Ringo as an individual as well as a performer I have to say I was impressed. He truly is one of the most gifted drummers of all time. There is no doubt about that. You would never realize that fact talking to him. He doesn't think of himself in that way. When he gives the peace sign and says, "Peace and Love" those words exemplify who he really is. He is such a gentle soul who just so happens to have also been a member of the Beatles. I always looked forward to seeing him in

145

concert. His concerts always give people a sense of belonging. His All Star Band always consists of some of the most sought out performers in Rock and Roll. All of them would never turn down Ringo if he asked them to be a part of his All Star Band. Everyone highly respects Ringo as both a performer and as a person. The reason is not what he represents as a member of the Beatles but who he is as a person. The fact he is one of the 'good guys' on this earth shines forth.

There was also another entertainer we saw at the Arena who had a profound impact on me for a different reason. Thinking back to when I was between the ages of nine and ten years old, my Uncle Irving would take me and my cousin Rob on his boat on fishing excursions. The name of the boat was the 'Buckeye'. It was an all wood boat that my uncle had bought after he came back from serving in World War II. It was my uncle's pride and joy and he took meticulous care of his boat. During the summer months my uncle would dock his boat in Woods Hole, Massachusetts and we would drive to get on the boat from Rhode Island. My uncle would plan fishing trips with several of his friends. Most of them were judges and lawyers from Washington D.C. and Virginia. We usually fished for Bluefish.

From Woods Hole, we would venture to Martha's Vineyard. Our trips would last three to four days at a time. There was another kid that always wanted to go along on our fishing trips. His name was Jimmy Taylor and he would stay with his family at a cottage they had, located on Martha's Vineyard during the summer months. I don't remember exactly how my uncle knew his family but they all were very friendly, nice people and they would invite us to sleep over at the cottage during our fishing trips. After fishing all day we would all retire to the Taylor's cottage to have supper before getting ready for bed. Jimmy's sister would usually play something on the piano while Jimmy played the guitar and sang a tune. Jimmy would make up his own songs usually songs with a folksy bluesy beat. We all would join in by either clapping to the beat of the music or harmonizing together. A great time was had by all.

Jimmy was tall and lanky and on the shy side. Jimmy was always whistling and singing some sort of song. I had a secret crush on him even though I was much younger than him. We all had so much fun on these fishing trips. I think my uncle liked having my cousin and I with him because he had no kids of his own and had never been married. My cousin, myself and Jimmy liked being included on these ocean fishing trips with my uncle and it made us feel like someone didn't just leave us behind because we were kids. We were included in the activities.

My uncle would teach us kids all about the mechanical parts of the boat including how to fix things that might go bad and how to drive the boat on the water. I had very fond memories of those years that I spent with my uncle, cousin, and Jimmy. After becoming a teenager I didn't get to see my cousin or uncle much because my parents were separated and later ended up divorced. It was a time of turmoil in my life.

As an adult, years later, I was offered tickets to see James Taylor in the Arena at Mohegan Sun. I tried to keep in touch with my cousin Rob as much as time allowed but we both had families of our own and didn't get to connect as often as we did when we were younger.

147

A few days before the concert I was talking to my cousin on the phone trying to catch up with what was going on in both our lives since we had seen each other last. I told him that Mike and I were going to get to see James Taylor in concert.

My cousin said to me, "Deb, don't forget to say hello to him from me. It should be fun for you to see Jimmy after all these years."

I was perplexed as to what my cousin was talking about. I asked him, "Rob, what are you talking about?"

Rob answered. "Deb, don't you remember Jimmy that we used to go fishing with?"

I said, "Yeah, of course I do, why?"

"That is James Taylor."

At that moment the realization dawned. My childhood crush was now a world famous singer/songwriter. I felt very silly I hadn't made the connection before now.

I said to Rob, "You mean Jimmy is James Taylor? Wow, I can't believe this never came up in conversation all these years until just now."

Rob then answered, "Yeah who would have thought he would have become a famous singer and songwriter years later."

Going to the concert a few nights later I felt excited to think that I might get to reconnect with Jimmy after all these years and maybe be able to reminisce about the past and all the wonderful memories. While watching him on stage I tried to remember him as that shy little kid I knew long ago. As I watched him I could see him in my mind as he was then. Seeing him now, I felt proud of him and all his accomplishments. I welled up with tears missing those few times when I was able to be just a kid as I now seemed to hold the weight of the world on my shoulders with all the responsibilities of adult life.

After the concert ended I tried to make my way through the crowd to the stage to speak with him. Mike told me to push my way through but there were too many people in my way. There was a wall of people crowding around him in hopes of getting his autograph. He was signing and talking with people but no matter how I tried I was unable to get through the crowd before he left the stage. Maybe someday I will meet up with him again.

As I continued writing in my journal I thought of a certain night when I met up with my friend Mark in the high roller Pit. Mark called me to come join him that night conveying to me that he was extra lonely that night and didn't want to play slots alone. Every time I met up with him he would ask me the same question before starting to talk about anything else.

He would say, "Do you know any girls my own age?" I would always tell him the same thing every time he asked me – I didn't.

I would look at him and say, "Don't worry Mark, there is someone out there for you. You will meet her when you least expect it."

We would also talk about the graphic art projects each of us were working on at the time. I remembered this particular night because as I was sitting there playing a three coin 'Wild Rose' five dollar machine and Mark was playing a two coin 'Double Diamond' five dollar machine. A very beautiful slender young woman with long dark hair came into the area. She sat a few machines from us and started playing a two coin 'Quick Hit' five dollar progressive jackpot machine.

I nudged Mark and said, "I think your dream girl has arrived."

Mark paused from playing his machine to look at her and then turning back to me like a scared little boy said, "Someone like her is way out of my league."

I tried to convince him to at least make some small conversation with her but he would not. I didn't want Mark to miss this opportunity if there might be one. I cashed out the $1,080 I had accumulated playing the 'Wild Rose' machine and went to sit and play the machine next to where she was playing.

There was one thing I had learned from frequenting the casino. I was no longer shy or afraid to talk to people. I smiled to invite a response.

I said "hi" to her as I sat down. She smiled back. She appeared to me as someone that was friendly and outgoing. I immediately started up a conversation with her.

"What's your name?"

"Susan"

"What do you do for a living?"

"I'm an art teacher at Three Rivers Community College. I just moved to the area from Oregon. I'm living with my grandparents until I can save up some money and get my own place." She smiled demurely as if that sounded a bit old-fashioned.

"This may sound a little bold", I said, "but I want to fix you up with a great guy I have known for a long time."

With a puzzled look on her face, she seemed to be mulling over the idea. It was hard to tell if she would go for it or not. I charged ahead anyway on a hunch she would.

I turned and called out to Mark saying, "Mark, I want to introduce you to my new friend Susan."

Mark, although blushing in embarrassment, cashed out of his machine and came over. Mark was a cute guy and I could tell by Susan's body language that she was very interested in him. Mark's warm smile through his mustache won Susan over immediately. Before long they were chatting and laughing and having a grand old time.

Mark found his dream girl that night. Eventually the two of them ended up moving in together. They became a closely knit couple and everyone that knew them could see how much in love they were with each other. They would act like school kids at times. The two of them would play their respective slot machines and then get up, join hands and sneak off to a corner in the lounge. They would start making out as if they were strangers meeting for the first time. It was game they played with each other.

In time Susan and Mark became a team in business as well after Mark asked her to come join him in his graphic arts studio. Even though they were now a couple, Mark and Susan would still want me to come join them occasionally in the high roller pit where I had first introduced them. The two of them were very romantic in that way. They would sometimes play the same machines they played the first night they met. They would call over a hostess and order a glass of champagne for everyone playing in that area. They would then raise their glasses and toast each other and the fact that they had found each other crediting me as

Debbie Tosun Kilday

the one that brought them together. It was a very touching scene and sometimes they would make me cry.

About a year and a half later I saw Susan playing alone one night and looking lost and forlorn. She was playing a Double Diamond machine off in the corner away from all of the other players. It seemed like she was trying to hide way. As I observed her from a distance, her right hand hit the spin button every minute or so; almost absentmindedly as if her heart wasn't in it. I approached her and sat down at the machine next to hers.

"Where's Mark? I haven't seen him recently." A feeling of dread came over me when I saw the tears starting to well up in her eyes.

In a meek voice that was barely audible she whispered, "Mark passed away last week."

She bowed her head in silence. The shock of her announcement hit me like a thunderbolt out of the blue. The tears were rolling down my cheek but I managed to force the words out.

"How did he die?"

"He collapsed while we were having dinner one night. I couldn't revive him. I called 911 and he was rushed to the hospital. He was diagnosed with a brain aneurysm. The doctors couldn't save him." She sank back into the chair.

I imagined her standing by his bedside in the emergency room. The doctors and nurses were probably crowded around his bedside working feverishly to save him; wondering what they could do next. She was sitting in a chair in the corner feeling helpless and alone in her grief. It made me feel worse. All I could think was that when a person was dying slowly like Kathy did, and

152

you knew it was inevitable she would die, it was painful to watch. However, it was expected. You could prepare yourself for the inevitable. When a young person like Mark died suddenly and unexpectedly it was truly a shock to the senses. You couldn't prepare yourself for that. All you could do was stand by helplessly, and wonder why did this happen?

I remembered a saying about untimely death but didn't recall who had said it. *When you lose your parents, you lose your past. When you lose your spouse, you lose your present. When you lose your child, you lose your future.* There was no real consolation for any of those losses. There was only the pain that followed. I supposed the grieving process in each case was a little different, but no matter you had to deal with it the best way you could.

I choked back my tears and tried to say the most positive thing I could to Susan. "At least you and Mark got to have some happiness if even for a short time. Life is so very short. You have to grab whatever happiness you can when it presents itself to you. I am glad you recognized that fact the first night you met Mark."

Susan turned to me and said, "Debbie, you are so right. I can't thank you enough for all you did for the two of us. I know Mark never forgot it. He would talk about it all the time to me."

The day finally came for my appointment with the 'Agency'. I drove to an official government building in the city. As these buildings often were, it was a towering structure of steel and glass, cold and uninviting. On the street the pedestrians hurried on their way to their own particular destination oblivious to those around them. I parked my car, fed the parking meter and went through the mammoth glass doors in front of the building. All the while I was hardly able to breathe or walk a straight line. A feeling of dread was beginning to overcome me as I climbed into the elevator and pressed the button for my destination floor. I tried hard to keep my anxiety under control so they wouldn't know I was scared to death. Getting dressed that morning I tried to look studious to appear confident I knew all my numbers were correct.

As I walked down the corridor, I looked for the number of the suite the meeting was to be held in. With each step my anxiety grew, fearing what would greet me there. When I got to the room, I took a deep breath and opened the door. Inside there were three people waiting for me, two men and one woman seated at a long table. The beige walls were bare. The only furniture in the room was that long table and a row of chairs lined up against the wall. One chair had been placed on the opposite side of the table top facing the three people seated at the table.

One of the men resembled and acted like the character Archie Bunker on "All in the Family." He was barrel-chested wearing a suit jacket that was half-a-size too small for him. His belly hung slightly over his belt. I imagined he didn't spend a lot on his wardrobe being he considered himself a hard-working guy who wasn't concerned about appearances. He looked like the no-nonsense type who demanded results, and wasn't too concerned how they were achieved. He observed me as soon as I entered the room with his elbows propped up on the table to support his weight.

The other man had dark brown slicked back hair, balding in the center, and wore a three piece suit. He reminded me of Richard Nixon because he had a ski-jump nose that protruded from his face with a thin, sarcastic smile beneath it. I noticed him making casual remarks to the woman sitting next to him that I couldn't hear. I imagined that this guy hated and blamed people like me thinking I didn't work for a living as they did, so I deserved to suffer at their hands. He wouldn't look me in the eye as I approached the table. He kept his eyes focused on the empty table in front of him.

The woman was thin and angular with eyes like an eagle which watched me intently. Her gray hair was pulled back in a bun with not a hair out of place. She was neatly dressed in a gray suit jacket and matching skirt. She appeared to be the studious type like a math teacher who graded fairly but always went by the book. She would be the teacher who assured a student always got the grade they deserved, nothing more, nothing less. The woman although courteous, had a stick up her ass so far I thought I could see the top of the branch sticking out the top of her head. After the three people assigned to my case made their introductions, they told me to sit down in the chair facing them, and immediately got down to business.

On the table in front of them I put my mass of records. As they poured through it, I could tell they were impressed with my meticulous record keeping. That did not mean they would allow me to get out of there without paying taxes on money I didn't win or no longer had. I didn't pay attention to the time and kept pushing my records in their faces while I incessantly talked. I didn't want to give anyone an edge for fear they would ask me a question I could not possibly answer. All of a sudden the woman spoke up. In a cold, foreboding voice she said.

"We will contact you with our decision, Deborah".

The fact she had personalized this inquisition by addressing me startled me a little. It was then that I glanced down at my watch and realized I had been there for four and a half hours. I shook each of their hands. I also thanked them for their time all the while thinking to myself there was nothing to thank them for or at least not yet. I had to leave all my files, journal, and W2G slips with them which I was not comfortable with. At the same time I was not going to argue with these people.

A few days later I got a call from their office telling me to come down and collect my records. At that time I would be informed of their decision in my case. When arriving at the office I told a receptionist my name and I was led to a room. I sat there for a half hour waiting for someone to come see me. I had the patience of a saint but this was ridiculous. All of a sudden the door opened and all three of the people I had seen before walked in. 'Archie Bunker' was holding a piece of paper in his hand which I knew held my fate. I tried not to look too concerned hoping for the best.

He then read from the paper. "Deborah, you are hereby notified that it has been determined that you have shown proof of winning $630,000 in Las Vegas and have paid the tax on that amount and have shown a detailed account of your winnings and losses. It is also assumed by the members of this team investigating your level of play that you may in fact have won much more than that amount. We have estimated that it is possible that you may have won another $350,000 during your time there. You cannot and we cannot show proof positive that you do not in fact owe that amount. You shall have sixty five days to pay a fine for possible undisclosed winnings in the amount of $60,000 to this office."

At first I wasn't going to say anything and just accept what was being said to me. Instead I spoke out and said, "I gave you people a detailed day by day account of my play. I have shown proof of all my wins and losses. I do not think you can expect me to pay any sum of money other than what I am responsible for."

Before any of them could come down hard on me I continued by saying, "Even though I do not agree with your decision, I will abide by it and pay the amount you are asking for."

After making that statement I picked up all my records, turned and left the office without looking back. I paid the fine the day before it was due and not one minute sooner. I wished this was the end of it but it was not. A similar situation would present itself in the future.

From this experience I came away with a lesson for all slot players: *The majority of people lose much more than they will ever win, especially playing slot machines. That is the normal outcome for people playing slot machines. Don't let anyone tell you that you can win huge amounts of money and just be happy about it. There are consequences, but only if you are really good at it like I am.*

16 – Forbidden Fruits of my Labor

After paying out sixty thousand dollars cash to the 'Three Extortionists' for the idea that I may or may not have made more money playing slots than what I had paid in taxes, I was really upset. I was upset about the way I was perceived more than the fine. It was assumed that because I was a gambler I must also be a liar and a cheat. Their perception of me made them think they could and should take advantage of me. The worse part about their perception of me was that they thought of me as one of them. Thinking back I should have fought them. Instead it was my conditioning from childhood to abide by the law that held me back.

I was taught that the people that worked for the government were there to help and protect the general public. I was taught to blindly respect them without taking into consideration that they too were people. The problem with that line of thinking was that there was no one to oversee the government employees. With no one to oversee the government, there were those that took advantage knowing that fact. The three government employees I had just met were indeed not good people. All of these flaws in how government worked without a check and balance was why there have been revolutions in the past.

All of the pressure from family either demanding perks or badmouthing me was getting to me and Mike. I had already learned that I was not that important to them unless there was some sort of favor provided by me. I was resigned to these facts. Mike was still denying them to himself. Both Mike and I are pretty easy going people but now the word was out circulating amongst casual friends that if anyone wanted to have a night out that they should seek me out. I definitely have more patience than Mike does and would just go with the flow most of the time as to not create any conflict. Even I have limits and now was fast approaching them. I was not able to just go to the casino and have a quiet time away anymore with close friends. I found myself making hotel reservations for people I hardly knew and meeting someone's niece to give her and her boyfriend tickets to a concert. It was getting way out of hand and I knew I was the only one to stop it.

One day I realized that I had never been to Elemis Spa myself yet plenty of other people had at my expense. The fact that I had never treated myself wasn't sitting well with me. After showering people with gifts, I realized there was no effort on their part to try to reciprocate. If they would have offered, I probably would have turned them down but they didn't try to make that effort. In fact they did not even act appreciative. The more I gave the more they demanded.

Some even had the nerve to be picky with their demands. One such 'friend' by the name of Tom complained to me saying that it was unacceptable that he and his girlfriend had seats in the third row instead of the first row at a Chicago concert they had been treated to by me. After hearing that statement I knew I had to start the weaning process immediately.

Debbie Tosun Kilday

"You don't have to worry about that ever happening again," I said.

He looked at me nodding his head up and down as if thinking I would now make sure he had front row seats. He didn't have a clue as to what was coming next. I was sick and tired of listening to that crap from ingrates. I was ready to lace into him. The feeling of being used and abused had been building up for months.

"I won't have you sitting in substandard seats so from now on there won't be any concerts for you and your girlfriend." When he opened his mouth to plead his case, I cut him off.

"Go earn your own money and perks from now on. Don't bother me anymore. It is over."

That was the last time I ever heard from Tom. Nellie would yell at me for allowing people to use me like that but I noticed that people were also using her too. People had herded towards the feeding trough, me and Nellie, one too many times and had become conditioned to become gluttons. I guess I must be blamed for allowing it to happen in the first place.

I am a very generous person by nature. I usually like to see the best in people but they always seem to disappoint and show their true colors. I am not sure why we both had put up with this kind of treatment for so long from others using us for their good times while we both struggled to keep the perks coming our way.

Maybe *it* was the fact that we both were paying so many taxes we couldn't enjoy the casino experience anymore. It took so long now to win a jackpot unlike before. We held hope that things would turn around so we could win substantial amounts like in the good old days. Even though Nellie and I shared the same birth

160

date we had different opinions about things at times. The stress was taking its toll on Nellie. She had not won a major jackpot in a long time. She buried herself in her CPA work during the day and frequented the casino late at night only.

Nellie and John had broken up a year earlier over his return to excessive drinking. I felt she had been too hard on him. He started drinking after finding out he had prostate cancer. He had to have his prostate removed so he and Nellie's sexual life was all but dead now. They remained friends but didn't go as many places together like before. I think it was really Nellie not being able to allow herself to love John for fear he would die and leave her alone like her husband had.

Nellie became obsessed playing machines waiting for the big jackpot. The machines she chose were not ones that would have won consistently even in the old days. I played machines that won small jackpots but nothing that would add up to what I was accustomed to winning. We both ended up playing the small amounts we had won back into the machines, because they just were not enough to sustain us. We both had to admit to ourselves that we were both just playing to play. I have always loved playing slot machines whether I was winning or losing. Even though I had gone to other casino's I always returned to Mohegan Sun. I was a loyal patron but now I felt like the management had turned its back on the very people that would never have abandoned them.

Every time I saw the tech people doing maintenance on the machines I knew it was not a good sign. We all found out we were right. Most of our friends either stopped coming to Mohegan Sun or went to Foxwoods trying to see if they could win more there. Now we were both at the breaking point. Something had to give.

Deciding to take matters into my own hands, I contacted the management in charge of the slot machines to have a discussion on how they were programming the slot machines to payoff. All of the players I knew suspected that the machines were being programmed to pay off less than before. It showed in the lack of jackpots we were all experiencing. I always had a good relationship with all of the workers and management at Mohegan Sun through the years.

There had been much downsizing of staff because casino revenue was not like it had been in past years. I had even lost my beloved host, Cash. I was assigned a new host by the name of Janet. Janet was a bitch that liked people to beg for comps. She acted as if she was using her own money and I had to remind her at times that it was my money not hers that had earned those comps.

The casino was like any other large institution, the rumors flew. You could pick up information from employees about the inner workings of the casino if they had a bone to pick with management as well. Through the grapevine I found that someone new had been hired to reconfigure the machines so that they would no longer pay out huge amounts but instead pay small amounts on a regular schedule. As far as I was concerned I felt they should have kept the older staff that knew what worked. Anyone that had played in past years, people like Nellie and I, could tell you that when it came to playing slot machines the regulars always kept playing. If they won a thousand dollars they played at least half if not all of that back in. If they knew they would win more, they kept playing and playing for hours on end. As in the case with all of my friends there were times we just stayed at the casino playing into the next day.

After taking a customer survey, I was told to contact a director in casino operations to personally express my views since I was a high roller. I will use the title 'SlotsMan' for lack of a better name. From the moment I met him I saw SlotsMan as a young son of a bitch trying to make his mark on the world. He was in his early thirties with gelled back spiky dirty blonde hair and a cocky attitude. He had no history with me or any of the other VIP players. He also had no interest in making contact with the players. They were only the people that supported his paycheck but he did not realize that. He met with me for the first and what turned out to be his last time. Upon shaking my hand and sitting down at his desk his demeanor showed me he wanted to make it quick so that he could get on with his real business.

"I really have no interest in this meeting", he began with an air of indifference. "My superiors told me I had to meet with you because you are a high roller."

The opening statement let me know this guy was not well-versed in the casino's policy of customer service. "I have been coming here for several years, and I know the slot machines don't win like they used to."

As I paused to take a breath, he casually drummed his fingers on his desk. "I've been coming here long enough to realize that the programming has been changed on all the machines to a point that it is no longer even possible to win any of the large jackpots listed on the top of the machines without playing in three times that amount."

His answer to me was, "So what? That will save the casino money in the long run. That is my job, to try to find ways to cut costs."

I felt anger rising within myself and forcibly blurted out at him. "What you have done here is chase out the regulars, the Sachem and Sagamore Players Club VIP members, and the people with the big money that consistently used to come to the casino to play. Instead of rewarding those people for their loyalty you have instead changed the programming and most of those people have now stopped coming here. All of that big money is gone now. The clientele you get now are mostly people that are new to the scene. Some coming for the first time and some bused in from other states for a day trip which includes free play and a discounted buffet meal."

Again his answer to me was, "So what."

I responded. "When you treat people that are loyal to your place of business without respect, they will eventually stop coming. I am speaking today for about eighty of those people. People that used to come here and spend on average over twenty thousand dollars at each visit. Those people used to frequent here at least four times a week. Out of the eighty I know, there are now only around six left from my group."

Slotsman replied sarcastically. "Well, tell me why they should matter to me?"

"They should matter to you because in prior years when I would come into this place during a weeknight the place was so crowded I had to wait for someone to get off of a machine. Now I come in here on any weeknight and it looks like a ghost town."

I went on to say, "Now I no longer come in here at all during the week unless there is a concert." He casually examined the back of his hand while I spoke. I was frustrated that he didn't see how the casinos actions were bad for business. I made one last appeal.

"Having the machines as tight as they are now with no hope of ever winning a huge amount you will bankrupt this place and the people that come here. If you continue doing business like that you might as well close the doors all week and just be open on the weekends."

Slotsman looked at me as he bit his lower lip looking like he was gnawing on a piece of raw meat. He was silent for a long time and then finally spoke.

"Well, this was a fun meeting. Let's not do it again."

"If you won't listen to what one of your most loyal and successful players have to say, then you will be the next one out the door."

As it turned out he was the next to be let go but not until the downward spiral he had created was already in motion and the casino's reputation had suffered. Most of the players I knew were now going to Foxwoods MGM Casino for both the shows and the slot machines. Most of them would tell me that the play was better there now and that the more famous celebrities were going there instead of Mohegan Sun. There was a lesson to be learned here.

17 – A New Chapter

One by one I started to detach the 'fleas' off of myself, figuratively speaking. When someone would ask for concert tickets I now told them that I couldn't get more than two tickets and Mike and I were going to the concert ourselves so they were out of luck. When people asked me if I could get them a room or pay for their dinner I told them I had used up all my points buying electronic equipment and giving them as gifts. If you want to see people turn on you, just take away all the material things you were providing for them for the last several years. At times their reactions to not getting their way was almost unbearable.

One such couple, the Kingstons, got downright hostile when I told them I could not get them a room for the weekend. Mike and I were in the casino and they sought me out. I didn't even know they were going to be there. They came up to me while I was sitting playing a slot machine and asked me to get them a room for the weekend. I looked up at them and then tried to explain to them that I was no longer doing favors for anyone. I figured I really didn't need to go into a whole explanation as to why. The two of them tried to make a scene in public thinking this would force me to give them their way. The two of them started to raise their voices saying I better get that room for them because they had come all this way in anticipation of spending the weekend. I in turn didn't waste any time. I immediately signaled to casino security cameras above with a gesture they had taught me to use if ever I was in trouble. As soon as they identified me on the cameras, security raced over to where I was and escorted a 'certain' couple out of the building.

18 – Is It Just Me?

I have always asked myself this question: *Is it just me that walks by a slot machine, looks at it, and sees the potential outcome of the next spin?* Much time was spent pondering this question. I must admit that thus far I have only met one other person at the casino that understood and saw what I see when looking at a slot machine.

His name was Jet. He was very handsome with his dark brown hair that looked almost black. His bright blue eyes lit up and sparkled every time he settled in to play his favorite slot machines which just so happened to be my favorite machines too. He owned his own bar in New Haven, Connecticut and he frequented the casino just as much as I did during the five year span. He would bring his different male companions along with him on most visits, but there were times he would prefer to be alone while playing. If he did bring one of his boyfriends with him he would always start his night the same way. He would send his companion away after giving him a few thousand dollars, telling them to return in a few hours. I never asked him about it but surmised that he kept his private life separate from his casino life as much as possible.

It was refreshing to meet someone I could talk with about slot machines and how they worked. We would talk for hours while we played. Mainly my message was:

Most people don't want to hear my crazy talk about how when the machine is about to pay out, the reels spin faster right before they hit. I can hear it and see it. I can only imagine others can't. There is a regular rhythmic spin all other times. When a machine starts hitting cherries you don't get much money, mostly only two dollars, but it is a preview of a win that will come next.

Jet knew exactly what I was talking about and embraced me when he first found out we both had this knowledge that neither one of us could explain. It was fun playing alongside him. He would point out that his machine was starting to hit cherries and that he would soon hit a jackpot. I thought it was great someone else could know this besides me.

We sat for hours playing side by side talking about the changes that had been made to the different types of machines. He noticed the machines had been fixed to limit the number of jackpots they hit just like I did. It was really no mystery to the longtime players because they had a history to compare it to.

On one particular night Jet started talking about the fact that it was much harder now to win big money on a dollar slot. In past years it had been almost effortless. Now you had to spend more money and you didn't get the return like before. Jet and I would joke how we must be the only two slot freaks in the world. It seemed to be true. Neither of us could explain why other people just didn't see what we saw. Everyone had a special talent or an affinity towards something. Jet and I just happened to be two people that had a different type of talent than most. It made both of us feel better knowing that we were not the only one. Before meeting each other we both had no one we could relate and express our knowledge to. Even though it was much harder to win at slots than it was in the past, Jet and I were still in the top one percent of big winners.

One night while feeling tired and needing some down time from the casino, Nellie called asking me to meet up with her. I told her that I just needed to have some time off from the slots. I found out very soon by the background noise that Nellie had called me from the casino. She had been playing the striker machine near the Cabaret Theater in the Casino of the Sky for nearly three hours straight and had not won a jackpot.

The voice at the other end of the line implored me. "I need my lucky charm to be playing alongside me. I can't win a damn thing here."

In the background I could hear the sounds of the machine she was playing. As I am always looking to challenge my skills at playing slot machines, I remembered the time when I had turned my back to a Bally's 2x, 10x, 5x machine. Using only my sense of hearing, I played the machine realizing I could hear the programming of the machine without having to use my eyes to look at the face of the machine. I had only played that way once which resulted in me winning a $10,000 jackpot. It gave me an idea.

"Nellie, are you game for a little experiment?" I asked.

Nellie replied without hesitation, "Deb, I'm ready for anything at this point I am so desperate for a win."

"Okay Nellie, this is what I want you to do. First, get off that damn machine you have been playing for the last three hours.

"Deb, are you fuckin' crazy? I must have played in around fifteen hundred dollars. I can't leave now when it's going to hit."

"Geez Nellie, I can't stand it. Do you want my help or not? That machine is not going to hit a thing. Trust me for once. Have I ever steered you wrong?"

I could hear Nellie grumbling in the background as she cashed out the small amount she had in the machine. She had told me it was around a hundred thirty dollars, give or take a few bucks.

"Okay, now go over to the two, ten, five machines. Out of the three in that row I want you to play the one that is in the middle in that row. Once you start playing it, make sure I can hear the machine as it spins. You can also tell me what you see on the first five spins."

I could hear Nellie putting her first one hundred dollar bill into the machine because of the sound and length of time as the machine recorded a hundred credits. I heard the first spin. I could not distinguish what I heard so I asked Nellie for a description of what she was seeing on the face of the machine. I could tell Nellie was losing patience with me asking her all these questions.

Impatiently she blurted out. "Deb, I see two 5's and one ten on the face except none of them are on the line. The 5 and 10 are above the line and then in the lower right hand corner there is a 2."

On her next spin she described to me again, only this time she was getting into the groove. "Deb, this time I see a 5 and another 5 and a ten, all below the line."

I reassured her, "this is looking good," even though I was listening in remotely.

Before her next spin, I said to Nellie, "Don't stop to describe it to me, just press the spin button." In the background I could hear the machine was running faster than before. That was what I was waiting to hear.

"Okay, now spin the machine as fast and as often as you can for the next three spins and on the fourth spin, cause an interrupt on the machine by taking out your Players Club Card."

I knew something was about to happen. "Are you ready to win? It is going to happen right....now!" I didn't hear the machine go off. I knew something had gone wrong. I yelled into the phone.

"Damn you, you never listen to me. Nellie, do it again only this time take your card out on the fourth spin."

This time, even though it sounded so fast I could barely keep up with the sounds. I heard the machine go off thus winning a taxable win. There was a commotion on Nellie's end of the line, and a flurry of voices I didn't recognize.

I could hear Nellie talking to the person in the row at the next machine saying, "I always doubt her, I don't know why. She told me to take my card out on the fourth spin and when I did, I won the jackpot."

Nellie finally came back to me on the phone. I think I had the patience of a saint at times. This proved it.

Before she could speak, I said, "Hey Nellie, I know you either won $3,000 or $5,000. Which was it?"

"How do you do that? Deb, I won $3,000. How did you know? Really, how did you know?"

I surprised myself at times. To tell the truth, I wasn't sure it would really work even though I thought there was a really good chance it would. As far as knowing it would be a win of $3,000 or more? That was guessing on my part because of the locations of the numbers and symbols earlier. I knew it would be a bigger win by the sound of the machine and the speed of each spin.

The bigger the potential win, the faster the machine spins, right before the jackpot hits. *Why did I tell her to cause an interrupt on the machine by pulling her card out on the fourth spin? Trial and error is my only answer.* When playing slots for the five years I experimented playing the machines all different ways. Some things sound crazy, but as I proved in this instance, it works ... most of the time. There was no guarantee that when Nellie didn't pull her card out on the first four spins that the second time she tried, would work.

I will go back to how I view things. *You must envision what you want to happen, be determined to make it happen, believe with all your heart and soul that it will happen and then make it happen by working hard. Most of the hard work I have been doing involves a lot of thinking. At times I am exhausted just thinking back to the different combinations of symbols and numbers and how the positions of them will affect the outcome. Some people think I must have a photographic memory but if I do I am totally unaware of it. As I watch the face of a slot machine and see the progression of the numbers and symbols passing by, it must be at a subconscious level that I see the next step in the process. I see it in my mind, but I could never remember at a conscious level and write it down, for instance.*

I was really proud of myself that I had coached Nellie remotely into winning a jackpot. This brought me to a whole new skill level of play. I never would have thought I was really capable of it, to be honest. You will never know until you try. I felt happy hearing her joy over the phone. I want only the best for my friends, especially my best friend.

I said, "Nellie, don't pick it all to hell. Just enjoy the win, but promise me you will cash out and go home now once you get paid. I didn't go through all that so you could play it all back in.

"Okay Deb, I will. Thank you, so much. I really needed this money. All I can say is, WOW."

"Please don't ask me to do this anytime too soon. My heart can't take it." It really was an amazing feat if you realized what was involved. I felt exhausted and stressed while waiting to hear that machine go off. One thing I knew for certain was: *I am way too sensitive to all these things, both seen and unseen, but it is what makes me good at this game of playing slots.*

Looking back at that moment in time I felt a multitude of emotions. I was determined, yet not completely sure I could accomplish the task. I set out to do what most would deem impossible, which is what made me all the more determined to do it. I didn't want to accept failure because of my concern for Nellie. I was driven to have her succeed so that she could receive the money she so desperately needed that night.

The lesson for the events of the evening was: *It all comes down to passion for what you do and the love of doing what you are good at. The other factor involved is wanting to do something to help someone else without wanting anything for yourself. It is recognizing the fact that at that exact moment in time it is not about me as much as it is about her. Sure, I could have used that money myself or asked her for half of the win but those thoughts never enter my mind. As in the title of Sting's song, "That's not the shape of my heart."*

Debbie Tosun Kilday

19 – Kept From What I Love

I will never admit to winning the Megabucks but I will admit to dreaming about it. I knew what the exact amount would be and even knew what date and night it would hit. I wanted to go play the machine that night knowing it would win. There was a circle with five Megabucks machines in it. I even knew which of the five machines would be the one that would win the 2.6 million dollars. Mike insisted we not go to the casino that night being we would be going to see The Who in concert the following night. I couldn't convince him that I would win the Megabucks jackpot no matter how I tried. He did not allow me to go by myself either. As usual I gave into someone telling me what I should or should not do to try and keep the peace. If I was not going to win it then I would at least have someone I know win it instead.

I called up Kathy's husband Ned and told him to go play the ten times Megabucks machine. He didn't really believe what I was telling him about the machine winning the jackpot that night but knowing my history he also did not want to take the chance of not going and playing the machine. Ned went to the casino and sat down at the ten times Megabucks machine. He called me from there after playing the machine for over an hour and then winning $2,000. I told him to keep playing the machine. He told me there was no way he was going to play $2,000 back in. He decided to get off the machine and go home after being paid the $2,000. What he told me was that he was satisfied with that kind of win. I begged him to reconsider staying but couldn't.

The next night as I walked into the casino with Mike to attend The Who concert, I didn't have to go see that the Megabucks had won 2.6 million dollars. I already knew it had won the night before. I walked over to the machines with Mike. The area had been roped off like it was a crime scene. Indeed the Megabucks jackpot had been won. More surprising to me was that there were a couple of people still there playing them.

I knew one of the people that was playing those machines so I went over to talk to one of them. A woman by the name of Pam that lived in New York that frequented the casino was sitting at the five times Megabucks machine. She started talking as soon as she saw me.

"I was here last night when it happened, sitting right next to the guy. A guy named Ned was playing the ten times machine. After winning the $2000 I overheard him talking to someone on the phone and arguing with them. Then he told them he was leaving. As soon as he got up from the ten times Megabucks machine I sat down at the machine and played in two hundred dollars and won $500."

She paused to take a sip of her mixed drink, and then continued the tale. "Thinking the machine would not win again I went back to sitting at the five times machine. That was when a stranger to the casino, a man in his early sixties then came and sat down at the ten times machine and started playing it. No sooner had he sat down he won the Megabucks jackpot. The amount was 2.6 million to be exact."

She threw up her hands, "Who knew?"

As she said it, I felt sick to my stomach. I had known. I couldn't put myself out of my own misery. Mike was standing at my side hearing this and I sensed he was feeling very badly about not trusting my intuition. A win like that would have changed my life and his for the better. Now it faded away just like the dream I had foretelling the jackpot before it happened.

We went to the concert and 'The Who' was really great. They played all my favorites and some tunes I had never heard before. I couldn't believe I could get over what had happened but I did. *I am not a stranger to disappointment in my life or loss for that matter. Life is not fair but no one ever told you it would be.*

A week after the 10x Megabucks machine had won the 2.6 million dollars; all of the machines in the circle were taken out and replaced with another type of Megabucks machine. Observing the new types of machines in that circle I never did see anyone win anything that would make playing the machines worthwhile. Maybe it was just sour grapes on my part but I didn't see the need to play a machine that didn't win at least a hundred dollars in the first ten spins. I decided not to even try playing the new types of machines and never even walked by to glance at them after that.

It was now five years since I had first stepped foot into Mohegan Sun Casino. I was starting to reflect back to my first visit there and how excited I felt when I won my first ten thousand dollars. I laughed to myself thinking that ten thousand dollars was a lot of money then but would never satisfy me now. Not that I would scoff at ten thousand dollars, I wouldn't. *It is the fact that ten thousand dollars doesn't go as far and buy as much as people think it does.*

I missed Kathy terribly and wondered why good people seem to die so young. I was feeling very sorry for myself and started walking into the mall. When feeling depressed I tend to spend more money. *People deal with things in different ways and that is the way I deal with my feelings at times. Does buying a new outfit, a pair of shoes or a music CD make you feel better?* I would have to answer: *Yes, it does help when you are down in the dumps. Does that feeling last?* I would have to answer, *No, it doesn't. It is just a temporary high before you crash back down to reality.*

This was one of those days. I walked into Spin Street and started looking at the DVD movies. I ended up buying six movies and two music videos. Wondering if I would ever get the chance to watch them I decided that didn't matter much to me. I then started heading towards the other side of the casino.

I never frequented the Earth section that often as I mostly played in the Sky Casino exclusively. It was a weird fact but certain people only played in certain sections and each and every time they went to a casino they went to their respective areas. I would have to admit that I was one of those people. I walked around where mostly dollar machines were located. I didn't recognize any of the people playing there. I felt very lonely at that moment. I didn't want to feel like I was amongst strangers so I started walking back through the mall towards the Sky Casino. I didn't immediately go to a slot machine to play.

I instead went into the Sachem Lounge to grab a bite to eat. Some of my friends were there and it made me feel better to see familiar faces. Mindy was there sitting with the two Yugoslavian brothers. I went over to where they were sitting to say hi and they invited me to sit with them.

The first thing Mindy said was, "My husband thinks I am at the grocery store but I came here."

She continued, "I did go to the grocery store so I am not really lying. I just hope that my milk doesn't get too warm before I get home. I wouldn't want to have to explain what happened to the milk to my husband."

I smiled at Mindy and the two brothers laughed. We all knew that Mindy was always at the casino and always telling her husband she was going to the grocery store. Some things would never change much while others would constantly keep changing. As I sat there at the table with the others my mind started drifting. I was half listening to the others as they conversed with each other.

I began to evaluate myself and the past five years I had spent frequenting the casino. I had to ask myself if it was all worth it. The answer was mixed. Not what you would call a definite answer. I considered that there was no definite answer to all things in life. In my own evaluation I came to the conclusion that there were more good times than bad times at the casino. The casino itself was my own personal haven. I could escape there, hide out there, and enjoy myself for the most part. The problems started when I started winning so much money I was no longer just in the background.

I was never the center of attention concerning anyone or anything in my whole life. After winning all that money I was the center of attention of the people I knew and even people I didn't know. I couldn't say that I didn't enjoy some of the attention I had gotten. I would be lying to myself if I said that. I guess it was either no attention or too much attention that had me wondering if it was all worth it. Too much of anything could sometimes be a problem.

So why was I still there after five years? Why didn't I stay on the Earth Casino side where no one knew me? The answer to that question was that I was lonely. I was lonely and needed people. I had friends there and sought them out just like on this day. Why wasn't I playing tonight? The answer to that question was that I was afraid to a certain degree. I would win and win again and then others would notice me. Strangers would crowd around me to watch the entertainment. I didn't want to be a sideshow of sorts to others. I was tired. I didn't want to be everything for everyone all of the time. *I just wanted to be myself and not have everyone expecting something from me. I just wanted to be accepted for who I was, whatever that was.* There were always such high expectations expected of me now. It was almost like I wasn't allowed to be a person anymore. For the past five years I had become something larger than myself. People wanted to watch the slot wizard win incredible amounts before their very eyes. I felt like a freak at times. Then again the casino was where I really wanted to be if given a choice. I felt confused.

"Mindy, maybe I'll see you another day. Now I am going out on the floor to play some slots."

"I'll see you, Deb," Mindy waved.

The two brothers made a move to get up and follow me but I motioned for them to remain. "I need to be alone tonight, guys, ok?"

It was a nice way of asking them to leave me alone that night. They abided by my wishes. My casino friends usually respected my wishes and I always appreciated that fact.

I walked out of the Sachem Lounge and headed towards the area of the Sky Casino that was near the Cabaret Theater. I was going to play machines that hardly ever win any jackpots. I knew I would just be wasting money by going there. I also knew I could just relax and play for a long time playing the machines in that area without drawing attention to myself as long as I wasn't winning.

I hated to admit this fact about myself but I just needed some down time by being left alone. Wasting money just for the sake of playing was not a good thing but that was the only way I would be left alone and knew it. I headed over to a Double Diamond machine. They were my least favorite machines because they did not win consistently and when they did win it never made up for the money wasted before a win. This time would not be an exception. I felt smug in the fact that I knew my machines, even the bad ones.

I put a fifty dollar bill into the machine to ensure my loss. *Fifty dollar bills make it harder to win because most slot machines are not programmed to recognize them.* I played fifty after fifty, hour after hour. I felt good even though I had lost close to $7,000. The only comments coming from others playing near me were remarks of pity because I had lost so much money. I was one of the masses of people the casino counted on to lose money.

They were totally unaware that I had planned and executed my actions deliberately. I felt somewhat guilty about wasting money yet felt at ease with my losses. I knew it was wrong to think in these terms so before going any further I switched to another type of machine.

I started playing what I called a Striker machine. The people playing around me started to turn their attentions toward me now. They had watched me pour hundreds and then thousands of dollars into the Double Diamond machine. Some players told me that I should not have left that machine because it was so filled with my money now that it would have to pay out. Considering my expertise I knew that wasn't the case but I kept that knowledge to myself. Instead I reassured them that I had a feeling that this new machine I was playing might hit something soon. As far as I was concerned I knew I was right.

When I first started playing the Striker machine I immediately noticed that the solid red seven was showing itself on the line to the far right. I knew I would be hitting at least twelve hundred dollars within my first ten minutes of play. The win came exactly eight minutes into my play. I tried to act surprised so the others that had been monitoring my play for the last few hours would not be disappointed.

My win was more than even I had expected. I had won a taxable amount of $6000. I was no longer seven thousand dollars the hole. I was only down by a thousand now. I knew I would make that up in no time but I tried to act humble just the same. *Did I appreciate this win?* No, I didn't. To me it was only money. I could make more and would. After getting paid I bid my fellow

Debbie Tosun Kilday

players goodbye and walked down into the high roller pit.

I walked over to the Quick Hit five dollar machines. Someone had just won two thousand dollars on the Double Blazing Seven version of the machine so I knew that I could not win the progressive jackpot of five thousand until the machine took back two thousand dollars from some unsuspecting victim. I started playing the five dollar Black and White Quick Hit machine. The progressive jackpot was five thousand forty three dollars. That seemed like a good number to start playing at. I knew that if the machine was going to hit the progressive jackpot it would do so soon. If it wasn't, I would instead win two thousand dollars. Either way I would be happy. Soon I started getting two out of three quick hit symbols scattered on the face of the machine. This told me that the progressive jackpot was going to be my win. After playing close to three hundred dollars in, I hit the progressive jackpot of five thousand eighty dollars. People that recognized me like Mindy and the two brothers started walking towards me to see what I had won.

Some had comments about me like, "Oh Debbie won yet another jackpot, good for her."

Some casual acquaintances didn't look so pleased. I was now up by close to four thousand dollars after taxes. I should have been happy but I really was not. Instead I was thinking to myself that I felt happier when I had been surrounded by the people that were losing in the other area I had played at earlier. I couldn't help thinking about the fact that I was able to play for hours even though I had lost money. I really was too efficient at this thing called 'winning'. Usually I would want to

184

keep playing but instead I said goodbye to everyone and told them I was going home. Some looked disappointed and some looked glad. They too had grown tired of watching me win.

20 – And in the End

Life is not fair. It could be if we were not human but we are. People just don't like it when other people are doing well. I would have been fine if I had been a loser most of the time. Others could have related to me. I would have been one of them.

At times I would play machines that didn't have any possibility of winning so that I could fit in. When I won lots of money I was hated and ridiculed and abandoned by family members. When I lost lots of money I got the same results. Some people were only happy when I won so that they could keep asking me for money. I always gave money away in those circumstances because I couldn't stand to see and feel the ugliness of greed. I wanted them to just take the money and get away from me.

Through the years I have tried to change the way I think of money. I view money as a tool to buy things that you may need at the moment. I don't look at money and think of how it can help me in the future. Just as in Kathy's case you do not know if your future is two minutes, ten minutes, or thirty years from now.

Some people hoard money to leave it to the other members in their family. I am not sure if that is a good thing as I think back to Aqua's son who had been taken care of all his life and didn't know how to make it on his own at all. I would like to think that I can someday come to terms with money. I am not sure if I will ever be able to accomplish that goal but I will try. I would like to be able to live a comfortable life yet still work hard at the goals I set for myself. Money is a strange thing for me. I am not sure I can fully explain my feelings concerning it.

To look on the positive side I feel gratified that I was able to help so many people pay for their medical treatments, medications, and just have some enjoyment in their lives by going to a fancy restaurant, seeing a concert, or going on a dream vacation. I was able to make those things happen for people. I brought comfort to them even if for a short time. I truly believe in trying to make dreams come true for good people. I never give up even in the face of adversity.

There are not many of us that get to fulfill the dreams of others. Long ago I had thought about the prospect of someday having enough money so that I could be able to help others as well as myself. I was able to do a little of both things. It is funny how people think of me differently now. Since winning so much money, I am thought of as someone beyond the reach of others. People look at me differently, think of me differently, and treat me differently as well.

I clearly remember the first time that I met singer and songwriter Barry Manilow in Las Vegas. Upon meeting for the first time we were both wary of each other. I was thinking that because of all his fame he was beyond just having a normal conversation. He confided to me after getting to know me better that he too knowing that I was a High Roller made him wary of approaching me and just having a normal conversation. People are just people when you get right down to it. We all have our plus's and our minus's. We all have our likes and dislikes. We all have flaws for sure. We wouldn't be human if we didn't.

I have often asked myself. *Why can't we just embrace each other for all of the reasons we call ourselves human?* I know I try to do that with others but they do not always do that with me. Most people have certain expectations as to who they want me to be for them. When I don't live up to what they perceive me to be in their eyes, they have no use for me because of their disappointment that they couldn't get out of me what they had expected. At times I am a disappointment to people because I don't want them to get used to the idea that they can depend on me forever. I would much rather they depend on themselves for the most part so that one day when I am gone from their lives they can survive without me.

21 – A Pro for Hire

As of this moment I am denying myself my heart's desire. I am denying myself my incredible ability to win large amounts of money playing slot machines. After winning over 1.8 million dollars in taxable wins playing slot machines within the span of five years, I stopped going to the casino. I am not saying this is a forever decision but it was and is my decision for now.

During the five year timeframe I met some of the most wonderful people at a most unlikely place, a casino. I cherish each and every friendship made there and also the relationships with the casino personnel. My time at the casino gave me something I had always been lacking in my life. It connected me to people and my winnings allowed me to help others less fortunate than myself. My time at the casino took away my fear that I would never be really good at any one thing in my life. I would like to say that I no longer feel alone but that is not true. Since not going to the casino, I am now disconnected for the most part from the friends I made there. I still talk to them on the phone and exchange e-mails but not being able to socialize with them in person puts my heart in a sad place. I miss seeing them and talking and laughing and even crying with them.

If Kathy had not directed me there I never would have met them in the first place. I am eternally grateful to her. On the other hand, I was used because of my ability and taxed to the point I thought I would lose my life. I became the focus of people that had nothing better to do with their time but try to make me suffer because it was not them winning.

For a time I felt relieved as if I had just retired and could rest up now. I started getting calls two days later from my casino friends asking when I would return. None of them believed me when I had told them I was going to stop going. Most of them seemed edgy when I talked to them as if they were going through some sort of withdrawal. Even Mike was acting like that. I told them all I had decided to take a break from the casino. Instead I would spend my time writing my story about the five years. I would also tell the stories of some of the people I had met while playing there.

My attitude became one of indifference. I neither was happy nor sad about my decision. I found it odd that I had no real desire to go back to a place I had spent almost five years of my life at. The truth was: it stirred up a whole trail of emotions, before, during and after.

After stopping my visits to the casino, I quickly found my life before those five years was returning to me. It was not a good life but I claimed it as mine just the same. Trying to live on my disability checks and Mike's pay was not enough to live on. We quickly were struggling again trying to make it from paycheck to paycheck. This fact made me even more determined to stay away. I figured this was what my family, friends and even my own husband had been wanting from me for the last five years.

Why not give them what they all want? I said to myself. *Would it make them feel differently about me, I wondered?* The answer was yes and no.

Most of them embraced me, inviting me back into the fold. Mike was happy about it. I wasn't. I didn't want to be in anyone's fold. I had outgrown their boundaries. I had become open to new experiences, moved forward and had grown immensely. Now I felt as if I was stepping backwards and being stifled. These people had used me up and then had spit me out without a second thought. I didn't trust them and certainly didn't need them in my life now. As usual I kept the peace by not saying anything. My way of having my say is writing this book. I am somewhat satisfied with knowing that I got it out of my system and out on paper.

The lesson here is to not allow others to control your life if you can help it. I allowed it to happen to me thinking I would somehow be accepted and loved by those I used to call family. I thought that was the only thing keeping me from them. I was wrong. The truth is they never really cared for me at all. That truth is a very bitter pill to shallow. I should have cut them off and out of my life long ago.

I have always had a natural affinity towards artistic endeavors. While growing up I was never allowed to explore or nurture them. As a child I would go down to an area of the dairy farm where I grew up where there was a natural red clay pit. I would spend hours there playing in the mud making beads for jewelry which I would dry in the sun and string together with my mother's sewing thread making a necklace for myself and others. Even my collie dog, Queenie, had to wear one of my creations as her collar. Queenie was my best friend and wore my creations proudly. I also made little tea cups and dishes out of the clay for my make believe doll tea parties.

Later as a teenager I broke away from family to go explore my talents that had been suppressed up to that point. My first job was as a dog groomer's apprentice. After learning that trade I made enough money to apply towards buying my own art supplies. It was then that I met my first art teacher, Miss Lillian. Miss Lillian was very eccentric in her methods of teaching. Her manner of dress was artistic in itself. As she painted on the canvas she would splash some paint onto a part of her clothing. After studying the splash she would then take a piece of her flaming coarse red hair and use it as her brush. Dipping her hair in the paint she created many a masterpiece on cloth. She would tell me the world was a canvas just waiting for a visionary artist to use all the tools available. She would challenge me to push myself to be better at everything I did. Now I can appreciate and praise her for teaching me to look beyond what you see with your eyes and to use your intuition to create what you envision in your mind. Miss Lillian nurtured and encouraged me to become the artist I am today.

I sang on weekends in a Rock and Roll Band that my then boyfriend Marty was in. The other members of the band were all male so I knew I was asked to join as eye candy to attract a crowd. Singing in the band exposed me to crowds of people and got me over my stage fright. I found that I possessed a very talented voice. I was as surprised as the other members of the band were. I have always loved all things that pertain to music but my newly recognized gift of singing made me feel free to express myself more fully with my voice. Little did I know that all these experiences were preparing me for my future.

My travels would introduce me to different martial arts. I started my study with Kempo Karate but would evolve from there. I would soon meet and learn from two Tai Chi masters, one in New York City and one in Boston. They both shaped and honed my abilities in the martial arts. At the same time they shaped me as well. They taught me to connect myself to other dimensions within myself. My ten years of martial arts training gave me my ability to not depend on the use of my eyes to see but instead to use my heart and have a passion for all I do in life.

In trying to analyze how my abilities while playing slot machines came to be, I would guess it had something to do with the types of training that I had. I am just an ordinary person who found they possessed an extraordinary ability. I think that everyone possesses these abilities too. The only difference would be that I was able to tap into my abilities because I looked beyond what others try to see using only their eyes.

I find it odd that because I was unable to make large sums of money with my art and photography I was told by my family not to pursue those professions nor was I encouraged to. After winning huge sums of money at the casino I was told to not pursue that avenue either because of the stigma attached to gambling. None of my family members wanted the embarrassment they thought I would cause them. It didn't make any difference if it was slot playing or drawing on a canvas. They were afraid to tell their friends I did either one of those things. I find their whole mindset bizarre.

I spend most of my time now photographing nature, writing, and being an artist working with different media types. I also do volunteer work for several non-profit organizations in my community. I am constantly approached by people wanting me to teach them my secrets to winning at slots. To this day I feel I did not appreciate nor did I realize the value of the money I was winning while playing slot machines. I never had any experience with managing money prior to my days at the casino. Perhaps my downfall was that I needed a money manager which at the time was nowhere in sight.

If I could leave you with any advice it would be this. Don't be afraid to say 'yes' to new experiences. Do not be afraid to be able. Whatever you envision you are capable of making happen. Be grateful for the opportunity. Do not waste one second to experience it. Don't let people hold you back for their own reasons. Life is short. For some it is shorter than others. It is out there waiting for you to seize the reins and experience it. The only question I ask you is: What are you waiting for?

Epilogue

After spending a year away from the casino, income tax time was fast approaching. I felt assured that this year there would be no drama and no huge taxes to pay. I had a very modest amount of W2G slips totaling twelve thousand dollars from wins the previous year. I felt relaxed and called our tax person to make an appointment to do our taxes. I was actually looking forward to doing the taxes. I felt that this year would be different. I would no longer be taxed like a millionaire and was hopeful that we might possibly get a modest refund check.

Two weeks before I was to meet with the CPA, I was going about my daily tasks. I needed to go get a few items at the grocery store. I was in the grocery store in the dairy isle when I looked up after putting a container of plain yogurt into my carriage. Someone was walking straight towards me. It was Taxman. I felt the blood rush out of my head and I felt dizzy. Was this just a coincidence? I knew it wasn't no matter how much I wanted to believe it was. That smug grin I hadn't seen in awhile was staring me in the face. Taxman didn't waste any time by telling me what was on his mind.

Taxman tried hard to appear conciliatory. "Debbie, I feel really bad about this but I am here to give you a message from the 'Others'."

I asked, "The Others? What others?"

Debbie Tosun Kilday

Taxman continued. "You know, your old friends, the three extortionists."

I couldn't imagine what further injustice I had to endure from them. "Oh God, don't tell me that. What do they want? I haven't been to the casino for a year now."

He answered in the calmest voice he could muster. "I know that you haven't been there because I have been monitoring you, but they don't believe it."

I wasn't about to be appeased by his feigned sympathy. "Let's cut to the chase. What do they want?"

"Deb, they want $26,000 in taxes they assume you owe. They think you still went to the casino after saying you stopped going. They are assuming you played without your card in the machines or used someone else's card instead to collect huge wins."

I said indignantly, "You know that isn't true. Why don't you stop them?"

Taxman pleaded, "I can't. This is beyond me. I tried, I really did. You know I like you. I tried Deb. I'm sorry you didn't take me up on my offer long ago. If you had, this wouldn't be happening now. If you would have cooperated with me you never would have met the three of them. Today I wouldn't be standing here giving you this news. Maybe we would be in some hotel room screwing our brains out instead."

At that moment thoughts of disbelief were racing through my head and I knew I had to get out of the store and get some fresh air, fast. I knew I would be on the floor passed out if I didn't. I was beginning to feel my chest tighten up and my stomach was starting to hurt. I felt like my ulcer had returned or I was about to have a heart attack. I left my carriage and the few items in it and headed towards the exit. Taxman was trying to

196

put his arm around my waist to support me thinking I would drop. I knew I was in trouble. I didn't want to lean on him but there was no one else. I found myself outside bent half over trying to get my breath.

I heard Taxman saying, "Take it easy." Finally, I gained control of my breathing. I was still feeling weak in the knees and lightheaded.

"They took the amount you won in taxable slips last year and more than doubled it. That is what they want."

I mustered my strength and lashed out at him. "I swore to myself last time that this would never happen to me again."

Taxman said in a soothing voice, "Deb, this time is different. You haven't even left the state to play elsewhere. Even I don't understand why they are doing this."

It almost sounded like an apology. From Taxman a hint of guilt in his voice was not something I was used to hearing, almost a sign of weakness. Now my initial fear was turning to anger. I knew what their game plan was. They wanted one last payoff before their cash cow was put out to pasture. I wanted to fight back but I wasn't sure who to target as my real enemies. Taxman wasn't the enemy, just the messenger. I did realize that Taxman didn't work for free though. I decided I needed to meet with the three once more, face to face.

"I need you to do me a favor and set up a meeting with them for me. I am not going to be bringing any money with me for them this time though. In fact tell them that, so they don't expect any."

Taxman said, "Okay, I'll do that for you but now you are scaring me. You aren't going over there with a weapon or anything are you?"

Instead of answering his question I started laughing like I had lost my mind. At that moment I was actually wishing I had so that no one could expect me to act sane. Maybe they would leave me alone if I was insane. I regained my composure and felt very determined and serious. *Maybe I am losing my mind*, I thought to myself.

I said to Taxman, "I'll be waiting for your call as to when I will be meeting with them."

Taxman said, "Are you okay?"

I answered, "Never better. Sorry about that little outburst earlier."

Looking at Taxman's face I knew he was scared both for me and of me. I didn't go back into the grocery store. Instead I got into my car and started driving home wondering what I should do next. I needed a plan but didn't have anything left. These people had taken everything good I had done for others and had reduced my good deeds into a cheap moneymaker for themselves. I was their victim once and here they were trying to rape me yet again. I didn't know what to do or where to turn for help.

Long ago when I was making and selling my handmade pottery to area florists, I encountered one customer by the name of Tommy that was a member of 'The Family' aka 'A La Famila'. I decided I would contact him to see if he could give me some advice. These three government employees were far more criminal than any Family members I ever knew. With the 'Family' they never treated you like these people had treated me. If nothing else there was never any doubt as to where you stood with them or why. They were straightforward people. I could respect that. The only thing I wasn't sure of was how I would contact him. It had been many years since I had sold pottery. I decided to go to where I knew there would be people that could help me contact him, City Hall.

I hate to suggest that you could get info on 'The Family' down at City Hall but it was true. Anyone that knew anyone could be found at City Hall. I ventured in there one day and spoke to one of the clerks asking if anyone knew how I could get in touch with Tommy. It had been years since he had retired. The clerk told me to go to the East End Firehouse and to ask for a man by the name of Bobby. Bobby would help me find Tommy. I drove to the firehouse and asked the first fireman I met.

I said, "Can you tell me where I can find Bobby?"

He said, "Who wants to know? " I immediately knew by his response that he must be Bobby.

I said, "Hi Bobby, I hate to bother you but I am an old friend of Tommy's. I need to find him so I can get some advice about a problem I am having."

Bobby looked at me cautiously and then answered, "Hey, I remember you from long ago. You're the pottery girl from the seventies, right?"

I said, "I can't believe you recognize me because I don't remember you at all."

Bobby said, "Maybe I can help you. Do you really need to talk to Tommy? He doesn't like being contacted since he retired."

I wasn't sure if I should be talking to this guy Bobby but he seemed like a good enough guy. I couldn't really be picky considering the nature of my request. I relayed the story about the notorious three and how they had collected money from me but I knew it went right into their pockets instead of towards any taxes. I told him of the situation pending and asked him if he had any advice on the subject.

He smiled a nice smile and with his thick Italian accent said, "Hey don't worry about it, piece of cake. I know some people that know of you at the casino. Let's just say we all have similar problems. I can help you out but you will have to go talk to them yourself."

Then Bobby told me who to contact. I thanked him and left. I made a call to the phone number he had given me and a man answered. He had already been expecting my call. That was surprising to me being I had just left Bobby less than three minutes earlier.

I thought to myself, *Wow these people sure work fast.* I was told by the person on the other end of the phone that I would be meeting several people to discuss and state my case. The meeting was the next day. They would then handle it from there whatever their decision was. There would be some "Family" members there but also some tribal family members as well.

I was well liked by the tribal members. They would sometimes come out onto the casino floor to watch me play as did other people frequenting the casino. The person on the phone then told me that we both had something in common. I asked what that was.

He said, "We don't like the government taking money that is rightfully ours and we don't like it when they screw around with us or with friends of friends."

"I guess we are on the same page then. See you at the meeting."

While driving to the meeting the next day, I was a little nervous only because I didn't know exactly what to expect. I tried to keep focused and keep my head together. Once inside the meeting place I felt relaxed. I saw people I knew and hadn't seen in quite awhile. It felt more like a reunion of sorts rather than what the meeting was really about.

After the initial introductions we all sat down. Once the meeting was in session they didn't waste any time getting down to business. At first I was told to tell everyone what the situation was concerning me. After conveying my story to everyone there, I sat quietly with both hands face up in my lap.

After much discussion amongst themselves I was reassured that whatever could be done to help me would be done. That being said one of the members announced that the meeting was over and it was time to eat. We all shared a wonderful array of buffet food items. I couldn't believe that I felt relaxed and was actually enjoying myself. I really missed the interaction with people. I had denied myself of the place I loved to be. My favorite activity, the thing that had given me such joy, playing slots, was replaced with the fear of hurt.

A few days after the meeting, I got a call from the fireman Bobby. He informed me that they had done the best they could for me. I asked him what that meant.

He said to me, "Instead of having to pay $26,000, we made a deal with 'them' to reduce the amount you will pay to $12,000."

I said to Bobby, "I had been hoping to not pay anything at all but I am grateful for the fact you were able to reduce the amount to less than half."

I thanked him several times before he finally said, "Enough already! We were glad to help. Take care Debbie, bye." He then hung up.

My situation was now half over. Even though the amount had been cut in half, I still had to face 'The Three' again. I also had to figure out how I would come up with the $12,000. my extortionists were demanding. After much thought I knew there was only one way I could come up with that kind of money. I had to return to the casino. There was no other way I could come up with $12,000 in a short amount of time and make that kind of money legally. My quandary was not that I could make big money playing slots. I didn't want to win huge taxable amounts that would generate W2G slips therefore drawing more attention to myself. Instead I wanted to win smaller amounts over and over. I felt very cautious as to how I would accomplish this. I wanted to just go in, win enough, pay off the sharks and get out.

I called my friend Nellie and asked her to come meet me at the casino. At first Nellie was shocked that I was going to the casino at all. After explaining the situation to her she didn't hesitate to come join me. I knew Nellie would never turn her back on me and would do just about anything I would have asked of her. She was my best friend and I could count on her help. I just wanted company was all. She told me that she had started seeing John again on a regular basis and I was happy about that fact. I was glad that the two of them had found their way back to each other. I was glad that I didn't have to worry about two of my most favorite people in the world having to spend their lives alone with no one to share things with. I didn't really need her to be there but I wanted her to be there with me.

There was no time to waste. I would either go early in the morning or very late at night. Nellie would meet up with me at whatever location I told her to. She sat at my side and we played side by side. We didn't talk hardly a word to each other but at the same time we were in tune with each other for some strange reason. I didn't want to be bothered or talked to. When I saw people we knew I asked them to ignore me and to not tell anyone they saw me there. My intention was to play only quarter machines or progressive fifty cent machines where the jackpot would not exceed $1199.00. I needed to make sure I wouldn't win taxable amounts. It took me several visits to meet my goal. I felt exhausted by the whole tedious process of making money for 'the Others' that neither deserved my money nor earned it. On one particular night I looked over at Nellie as she played a machine for me. She was silent and totally engrossed in what she was doing. I was glad even now during this predicament that I had taken Kathy's advice six years ago and had gone to Mohegan Sun and made new friends. If I had not done so, I never would have met Nellie and the other people that were so much now a part of my life. Nellie was a true friend.

I made one last trip to visit 'the Others' and paid them their money. Upon entering their office I neither answered them nor spoke. I threw an envelope on the table containing the money. Around the envelope were several rubber bands wrapped around to hold the money in. On the outside of the envelope I wrote the amount of $12,000 along with a comment scribbled next to the amount.

On the envelope I wrote, "No more money shall pass this way again." I turned my back on them and started to walk away towards the exit.

One of them yelled out to me, "Go do your taxes now and we'll let you keep whatever refund you get." I kept walking towards the door and left their office.

Hearing that comment about doing my taxes after giving them twelve thousand dollars in cash made me convinced that these three people were criminals and scam artists milking the general public for their own gain. The problem I had with it was the fact they didn't even try to hide it. This made me realize that they did this sort of thing more often than not. It went beyond reason to have known that there was no one trying to stop them.

After meeting with our CPA to do our taxes, I found we would be getting a modest refund from both the state and the federal government. A thousand dollars from each would help us immensely. *Could this nightmare really be over*? I thought to myself.

I guess as it turned out, it wasn't over. The weeks passed as we waited for our tax refunds. Nothing came in the mail. After almost three months still nothing. Finally one day a letter came in the mail. It was from the office of my three extortionists. The letter didn't say much except that whatever refund we thought we would be getting was taken by them toward taxes we might owe.

I had been thinking of my next step for some time but before acting on it I wanted to see my friend that worked as a tax auditor for the State. I called my friend Matt at his work number and asked him if he would meet me on his lunch break. Matt told me he would be more than happy to help me with any advice he could provide.

I met Matt in The Capital near his office building. Upon seeing me he started to shake his head as he walked towards me.

He said, "Debbie, I can only imagine what has been happening to you since I last saw you. How are you doing my friend?"

I wanted to break down but tried to keep up my strong appearance as best I could. I choked back my tears so Matt wouldn't see me falter.

"I paid my extortionists the money I knew I didn't owe plus I know for a fact it went straight into their pockets not anywhere else. Now after months of waiting for our tax refund I got this letter from them saying they are taking the refund for possible money owed to them."

When he heard that the extortion was continuing Matt rolled his eyes. Without hesitating, he shot back. "Deb, you must stop the flow of money into their pockets. There may be only one way to do that. You are not going to like what I suggest to you, but please hear me out."

"How can I do that when I already stopped going to the casino a year ago and they still collected money I don't owe a year later?" I feared what was coming, but I also knew I couldn't allow the extortion to continue. Matt was right. It would never end.

Like he was reading out of a playbook, Matt rattled off his instructions. "Deb, start by draining your checking account but do it at an ATM machine inside the casino. Take cash advances from every credit card you own, again at the machines at the casino. Become a loser as fast as you can for as much as you can. Don't pay the credit card bills when they come in. Let everything crash, it is your only hope from getting out

Debbie Tosun Kilday

from under their grip. They can't ask for money legally if you don't show any legally. You aren't going to like where I will tell you to go from there but in about three to six months go see an attorney and talk about bankruptcy."

"Oh my God! Is that my only choice? Please don't tell me it is. I beg for you to suggest something else."

The very idea was bringing on a panic attack. It was contrary to everything I believed in. I am a proud woman and bankruptcy would have never come to my mind. I always paid my bills on time even when I didn't make much money. This was hard for me to hear and harder for me to shallow. I sat there looking at Matt's face and saw his honest concern for me. At that moment I knew I had to take Matt's advice. I didn't want to admit to myself that it was the only way but I knew in the back of my mind it was. *If the 'Family' couldn't stop them completely why would I think I could?* I had just paid those bloodsuckers twelve thousand dollars and they still took our refund check.

"I know in my heart you're right—but I wish there was another way." I pleaded.

Matt put his hand on my shoulder to console me. "There is no other way; not that I know of."

"Thanks for being my friend—when should I start?"

Matt was ready with further instructions. "You are halfway there being we are in The Capital. Get in your car and drive to one or both casinos right now. My guess is you don't have much time before they send Taxman again. Now that they have gotten their way a couple of times you will now have to stop them legally. Once you are in bankruptcy they can't and won't want to touch you. People like them can't afford to be noticed

206

by going after someone in bankruptcy. That status will protect you. Be strong my friend."

He gave me a good luck hug. As Matt walked down the sidewalk back to his office, I called after him, "Thanks again." He turned and waved.

While driving up toward Ledyard all kinds of crazy thoughts were going through my head. In the next few weeks I started draining our accounts one by one using the ATM machines in both casinos. I even wrote checks at the cages. Mike already knew we didn't have much money but now he noticed we didn't have any. I kept this painful secret all to myself. Mike started fighting with me about the lack of money and couldn't understand my interest in going back to the casino especially with my sudden downward spiral at playing slots. He also couldn't understand why I was still winning but would then play every penny back in and lose it all. No one could understand my erratic behavior. I was acting out of character. I knew I had to be convincing knowing I was being watched. This was not a game. It was an attempt to save my life by ruining it first. Most thought I had lost my mind. My marriage was now in trouble but I still kept silent. The only person I told was my best friend Nellie. She was my one true friend that would keep my secret. Of course Matt knew but it was his idea. I was confident that he would never betray me either. I didn't want Mike involved in this. It was the only way I could protect him.

I had to consider my next decisions carefully before acting upon them. I met with an attorney and he was very helpful with answering my questions and concerns. The one thing I was sure of was I had to stop the flow of money so that Taxman and the Extortionists wouldn't be able to touch me. The decision to bring to light illegal activities by government employees to an attorney was not an easy one nor was signing my name to papers to declare bankruptcy. For the time being though, it seemed my only option.

From my first meeting with the attorney it was now eight months later. During those eight months my attorney realized that without Mike's paycheck I could not declare bankruptcy by myself. He told me bluntly that without my casino income I couldn't afford to live, never mind pay any bills. My attorney was surprised that I was able to pay him the $3,800 he asked me for his services.

At my first meeting with him he had told me he would charge me no more than $1,200 knowing that things were tight without my casino income. I knew now that what he had first told me was a lie. He was depending on me to go back to the casino so that he could keep getting more cash as time went by. I told him how I had to borrow the money from a friend to pay him his fee. It was the truth but I knew he didn't believe me. I had to remind him that was my reason for declaring bankruptcy in the first place. The fact was that I did not make enough money to live on with my disability check. Even though I was told repeatedly that I shouldn't make any trips to the casino I was sure now that both my lawyer and the trustee assigned to my case were disappointed in the fact that they could not get any more money out of me. I was not cooperating by being their cash cow too. I thought my three extortionists were bad enough but now my own lawyer was doing it to me too. The trustee talked to my lawyer and told him that he needed to have Mike sign papers to be included in the bankruptcy along with me.

I tried to convince my lawyer that Mike should not be involved but it was to no avail. Mike reluctantly signed the papers but he didn't like it one bit. He told me that he didn't want to sign but felt he had no choice in the matter. He asked me repeatedly how this could have come to be in such a short time.

Any love that Mike may have felt for me in the past was replaced by indifference. He didn't love me or hate me. It was worse knowing that he now felt neutral toward me. I didn't think his attitude was really justified. I used to think that when two people were married that one should want to stand by the other in good times or bad. It really didn't matter now as to how Mike could turn his back on me so quickly. There were no answers as to why. What it showed to me was the power that money had over people. The greed factor ran rampant in all types of people in all levels of society.

As matters progressed, Mike was instructed by the trustee to pay him four hundred dollars a month plus pay our monthly bills. I wondered what had happened to all the promises my lawyer had told me about on my first visit. All the terms had now changed. Instead of erasing any debt we were now paying more each month than before. At the start of our five year plan the trustee decided that instead of four hundred dollars a month he would now take four hundred dollars bi-monthly.

While I was protected from the extortionists after declaring bankruptcy, it appeared the bankruptcy process was going to bleed us dry. I began to see how the system worked. I found out that the extortionists had taken our tax refund checks when they were not supposed to be able to. Technically that was considered illegal. However when the bankruptcy process did the very same thing that was considered legal. It seemed there was a fine line between what was considered legal and illegal. It depended upon who was doing it and why. I realized then the powers-that-be had you coming and going and there's nothing you could do about it. I also learned that the economic pie that people showed on graphs was for real and everyone wanted a piece of it. Whether that was fair or not that's the way it is.

Whenever you got scammed and they got caught at it, it seemed there was someone else ready to take their place in line. The bankruptcy process was merely a device to keep creditors in an orderly line. It was all under the guise of protecting you from them. When creditors became scammers, the question was: *who are they really and who is going to protect you from them? I don't dare to answer that one.*

My experience with the extortionists had exposed the seedy underbelly of corruption I never expected to be involved in. Because I made it extremely clear that I would not testify in court, I had no legal recourse. Without my testimony they got away with it. There can never be full disclosure. I didn't want the added attention plus if I were to testify I would then have to be put into witness protection. I didn't need any more drama in my life. I have had my fair share of it to last me the rest of my life.

While it is a noble goal to stop the corruption of federal, state and municipal workers who take advantage of everyday people, people like me and you, I expect the practice will go on I am sorry to say. The reason is most people cannot help but to take advantage.

ff here

There is always an opportunity for people to show compassion for those who are in a bind instead of driving another nail into the coffin. Whether they take it or not is a matter of choice.

The main difference between the poor man and the rich man is the depth of their indebtedness. That indebtedness is measured by the cost and quantity of their things. The richer you are the more things you have and the more expensive they are. No matter how rich you become, you will always owe someone. I found out the hard way that someone is the taxman. Whether you are rich or poor you have to deal with it.

No one knows, especially me, what the next chapter of my life will hold. My advice to others is to not allow what has happened to me to happen to you. How that can be accomplished when you win as much as I am able to win at just playing a slot machine is the challenge you must face.

Even now, *I am not afraid to be able.* Maybe I should be but I am not. I must add that this experience has been a real eye opener as well as an education for me. Money brings to the surface the true meaning of what people value most in their lives. The sad fact is most people do not value love or friendship. They don't seem to believe that leads to happiness. What they want most is more money and more things. They think that money will cure all their ills and more material possessions will make them happy, but I know firsthand that it will not. As in the title of Sting's song: That's not the shape of my heart.

As for those who aspire to be rich, I have the following advice. It comes from Lee Held. He says, "Being rich has nothing to do with money; it has everything to do with your heart. Money is just something you need to live on; your heart is what you need to live. Open your heart and find your truth, see the beauty of you hidden inside. See with your heart, respect with your love and be true to yourself, you are the beauty of life, give to live."

Let me end my tale with a quote from Abraham Lincoln. He said, "Folks with no vices have very few virtues." I think that is a lesson for all of us not to judge a book by its cover. We all have good points and bad points. The goal of one's life is to make those good points shine through in spite of the bad points. If you can say at the end of your life, "I did the best I could with what I had to work with", I guess you could do no better than that. You'll always have hope when you don't deny your heart's desire.

Anthony Curtis's Las Vegas Advisor Question of the Day

No part of these answers may be reproduced or utilized in any form or by any means, electronic or mechanical, without the written permission of the publisher: LasVegasAdvisor.com and Question of the Day, Huntington Press, 3665 Procyon Avenue, Las Vegas, Nevada 89103

Each one of the following statements was taken from *Anthony Curtis's Las Vegas Advisor Question of the Day* on the dates indicated.

Question of the Day June 9, 2007

Q: Why are we so hooked on slots?

A: Slot machines and video poker in particular – have been described as the crack cocaine of gambling. The analogy, while somewhat pejorative, is not without some substance. Cocaine was once primarily an expensive "status" drug, whose high price tag precluded mass usage. Similarly, before the advent of slot machines, casino gambling (as opposed to sports betting and other forms of wagering) was generally something of an elitist and highly male affair, with urban casinos (as opposed to the riverboats, which were less upscale) often consisting of salons and private members-only clubs of the dress code and velvet drape variety that are still found throughout Europe.

While the advent of cheap and plentiful crack democratized cocaine usage, slot machines accepting denominations as low as pennies, housed in large respectable but anonymous casinos, have opened up gambling to everyone, particularly women. Solitary and, in the case of slots (not video poker), requiring little to no skill, electronic games are far less intimidating than table games. The lack of social interaction makes it easier to lose track of time and become "lost" in the game, which for some can become a mind-numbing form of escapism.

And the parallel doesn't end with accessibility. The purity of crack and the fact that it's smoked rather than snorted means not only that the high is faster and more intense, but also that the feeling of euphoria is shorter-lived and the following depression and risk of an ensuing cycle of addiction all the stronger. Similarly, problem gamblers who regularly play slots and video poker appear to progress into pathological gambling much faster than those who only gamble at, say, horse racing, or other forms of gambling that do not have such an immediate rate of gratification.

The factors that influence what seems to be a strong relationship between gambling machines (particularly all forms of video gaming) and problem gambling are still not well understood, but anecdotal reports indicate that one risk factor may be the speed of play. In other words, the faster the wager-to-response time with a game, the more likely players may be to develop problems with that particular game. It's common for pathological gamblers to explain that it's the rush of being "in action" that's addictive, rather than the winning (which is often perceived as a good thing not in itself, but only in that it prolongs the ability to stay in action). Unlike betting on a football game where the outcome remains unknown for hours, or sitting at a full blackjack table where you have to wait your turn to play, slots and video poker rapidly and repeatedly deliver lots of little "highs," and that's what seems to get many people hooked.

There's also a physiological dimension to gambling addiction that's not fully understood, but which has been highlighted by the recent discovery of a seemingly bizarre correlation between people being treated for Parkinson's disease and various forms of compulsive behavior, including the sudden onset of gambling addiction in people who might never have gambled before in their lives. Parkinson's is a degenerative disorder marked by the death of particular brain cells; it's primarily treated by drugs that restore or improve neurochemical signaling systems that are dependent on the neurotransmitter dopamine. Dopamine influences balance and movement, but also mood, behavior, and the sensation of reward. The disease is treated with dopamine agonists, which bind to the dopamine receptors in the brain, and it seems that it's the possible over-stimulation of this part of the brain that can lead to more impulsive behaviors and produce a feeling of euphoria from activities that might have been of no interest or even undesirable before, such as gambling or alcohol consumption. While the study of this effect is still in its infancy, it may lead to a much better understanding of the physiology of addiction and in turn help to find a new cure.

Question of the Day July 9, 2008

Q: Your news section has mentioned a "leap forward in server-based gaming" and that "IGT has been contracted to create an all-server casino." What is a server-based casino? How would that affect the player and gaming as we know it?

A: In 2005, game consultant Rob Fier told the *Las Vegas Business Press,* "He who controls the wire controls the gaming floor of the future." The "wire," in this quote, refers to the networking cable that connects slot machines to a central computer system. Today's slots all have their own central processing units built in; to change a machine's games, denominations, and payback percentages requires manual manipulation of the machine itself by a slot technician. Tomorrow's machines will be client terminals dressed up in slot cabinets into which, with the click of a mouse, different games, denominations, payback percentages, bonuses, promotions, etc. can be downloaded from a single server.

When MGM Mirage opens Aria in late 2009, all slots and table games will be networked into such a central server. In many cases, the games will actually be mounted on this server and the "slot" machines will be more like what even Nevada Gaming Control Board (NGCB) Chairman Dennis Neilander has called "dumb terminals" into which you download the game content of your choosing.

"Every casino wants their floor to be dynamic," writes Aria President Bill McBeath. "You want frequent visitors to be able to see new product each time they visit and you want to make available the games that are going to be of interest to the people on your property at any given time. We learn from our customers all the time about their likes and dislikes. This technology allows us to respond to those quickly. For us, that is the most important reason for introducing this kind of technology into our properties."

Seeking a more detailed explanation, we turned to syndicated columnist and slot expert John Grochowski. "First, it will enable operators to tailor their games to player preferences," he replied. "If their databases show them they need more video poker during the day, but can fill with video slots at night, they'll be able to do it.

"Or," Grochowski continues, "if weekday crowds prefer penny games with more volatility and free spins, while weekend tourists like nickel games and second-screen bonuses, operators will be able to adapt quickly."

As Bally Gaming's Marcus Prater told the *Business Press*, operators could simply alter the denominations of machines, turning quarter slots into half-dollar ones on a busy Friday night –- all across the slot floor with but a few keystrokes.

IGT Vice President of Marketing Ed Rogich provides yet another example. "Tournaments today, you have to hold them in a separate area." With server-based slots, the games could be switched out so that you could play in the tourney without leaving your preferred machine.

Debbie Tosun Kilday

Likening many of the aspects of server-based gambling to player tracking, Rogich says, "Basically, it's a networked [system] that will allow the operators to manage their floor and provide communication to the players. [Also] it will connect the player to systems that already exist" and increase the number of possible offerings. "This is going to bring a network of systems and services to the players at each of it slot machines," Rogich adds. He likens it to the Internet, integrating many systems already in existence.

This is especially true of games. Because slot-game manufacturers will have to share sensitive game-code information to make this work (and, for once, the casinos are calling the shots here), IGT and Bally and Aristocrat games, for instance, have to be cross-compatible with virtually every machine on the floor. The player will have not dozens but hundreds of games from which to choose in a single slot session. Rogich likens the experience to downloading three movies from three different distributors. "Does that mean you have to have three different computers to download to?" The answer, clearly, is no.

You may have even played a server-based machine already without being aware of it. According to Rogich, IGT's downloadable slots are currently undergoing field trials at Treasure Island, MGM Grand Detroit and at Barona Valley Ranch Resort, creating what Rogich calls "the various iterations" of what IGT hopes to deploy at Aria.

In the past, our attempts to see the downloadable slots at Treasure Island have been rebuffed, with both MGM and IGT executives insisting that one wouldn't even be able to tell the difference between a regular

218

video slot and a server-based one, even if you were standing next to it.

Rest assured, the traditional reel-spinning slot is unlikely to go away. According to Fier, video-based games have tended to briefer life cycles than your good old Double Diamonds machine, which may have been out on the floor 15 years or longer and whose ilk will continue to represent a significant percentage of the slot product out on the casino floor.

But for the casino operator and slot provider, server-based gaming means a lot of saved time and manpower. Whereas now, making changes to a (for instance) Reel 'Em In game means having technicians change the EPROMs – the programming chips – in each and every machine, now it can be done with a few pushes of a button in a control room that runs the entire casino floor. Thrift, Horatio!

According to *Forbes*, "Business on these [downloadable slots at Barona] is projected to improve 25% over the usual take, says the casino's hired consultant." The article goes on to note that by identifying where the hot pockets of play on the slot floor are, it will be easier for casino operators to spot top-performing machines – and top players, too.

But we suspect what you (and many others like you) are wondering about, is how the ability to change games with a mouse click or two will affect hold percentages. "The instinct, from Bally's perspective, is not to change hold percentages," said Prater back in 2005. "That's not a good idea. Some players have a paranoia that operators seem to be changing hold percentages on the fly." (Indeed, one of the most persistent urban legends of the casino business is that swarms of slot technicians are sent out every night to go from machine to machine, tightening the "hold.")

They'll certainly have that capability. "Operators will be able to change payback percentages as well as games and denominations fairly quickly," notes Grochowski. "It's up to operators and regulators to make the process as transparent as possible to ease the fears of customers. In Nevada, and I think every other commercial gaming market in the U.S., operators will be prohibited from changing anything about the game while it is being played. If you're playing a 97% payback game, it's not suddenly going to become an 88(% game) while you're playing."

"Assuming that the software's been approved," elaborates the NGCB's Mark Clayton, "the machine must be idle for four minutes at a time," while its hold, denomination or content is being reconfigured: "No credits and no players' cards in the system." What's more, the machine's video screen must display a modification-in-progress message, followed by another four minutes of 'down time.'

"I doubt operators will be changing payback percentages willy-nilly, having higher percentages on the same game and denomination at one time than at another," resumes Grochowski. "However, when they change a nickel game to a penny game, you can expect the penny game to [be] a lower percentage than the nickel one."

Game manufacturers and casino operators prefer to emphasize the marketing and enhanced-entertainment possibilities of server-based slots. As one MGM Mirage exec told Forbes, "The next phase is the marketing aspect, talking one-on-one with the customers."

The way Rogich puts it, there is currently no good mechanism available for contacting players in real time, but server-based slots will allow that to be done while the player is at the machine. For instance, if you've earned a free buffet or discounted show tickets, a message can be sent straight to the slot at which you're playing. This eliminates the delay, hassle and mailing costs involved with sending out frequent-player rewards by mail, to be received several days after your casino visit. Such immediate gratification would have obvious appeal to players visiting Casino X from out of town, even more so than for locals.

The application of server-based technology to table games is considerably more limited. You can't turn a blackjack table into a craps one by clicking on a few links, obviously. By adding displays and interfaces, though, one could do the same kind of customer outreach as is being contemplated for slot, though. "The game would stay the same," concludes Rogich, "but there's ways that they can automate the table so they can track the play" using radio-frequency-tagged chips of the sort that are already in play at casinos like the Hard Rock.

Will customers go for this? As Raving Consulting President Dennis Conrad is fond of saying, "Nobody understands the slot player, including the slot player." But, as game manufacturers repeatedly point out, gamblers took to ticket-in/ticket-out slots faster than expected.

Still, the casinos haven't yet managed to put the downloadable-game technology on the floor, save for isolated beta tests. Those familiar with the ballyhoo preceding downloadable slots had to smile in recognition when *Las Vegas Review-Journal*'s Howard Stutz wrote, not long ago, server-based gaming seems forever to be 'one year away.'

Question of the Day June 12, 2008

Q: Concerning slot machines. Do you think it is possible that some slot machines DO NOT have the highest jackpot combo in the chip? They could pay 200, 400, or 1,000 units, etc., often, but never pay the big one. How would anyone really know? Are the chips checked for this?

A: For this answer, we turned to our deep-throat casino manager Arnie Rothstein, who deals with the paperwork generated by this very question for hours every day. Take it, Arn.

A slot machine's EPROM (erasable programmable read only memory) chip is preinstalled when it's manufactured at the slot machine factory. The customer (the purchasing casino) has numerous options to choose from that pertain to the "hit frequency" (how often a winning combination comes up on the machine) and "payback amount" (the percentage of coin-in that the machine returns to the player).

All machines come from the manufacturer with a "PC sheet." The slot maker prepares the sheet, which contains information about the make, model, pay table, amount of pay stops, frequency of hits, reel strips, theoretical hold, and other data on the machine.

Most casino jurisdictions require that the casino maintain a PC sheet for every slot on the floor. Nevada casinos are required to make frequent slot audits, which the Gaming Control Board reviews at will. (All casinos and gaming manufacturers and suppliers are audited by their respective control agencies.) Casinos regulate their machines and investigate any machine that deviates from a certain range of expectation, also known as a Volatility Index. (To calculate a slot machine's VI is a long drawn-out mathematical process, but it's accurate to within thousandths of a percentage point.) Some casinos have the technical ability to reproduce a damaged EPROM chip. But these chips must have Gaming Control approval, since all EPROMS have serial numbers and long paper trails. You can see evidence of how involved the EPROM process is when a major jackpot is hit.

Let's say I'm your lucky charm and after reading this, you go out and line up three Megabucks symbols. You'll immediately see the floor come to life. Security guards and floor people will watch the machine. Slot techs, a member of the slot manufacturer's team, and a surveillance agent will be present to see the machine being opened. The EPROM will be tested by both the house and surveillance and the serial number verified. Then, and only then, will you be paid.

So, turning to your question about slot machine chips that disallow the big jackpot. Can this happen? Sure it can. In the good old free-wheeling days, when casinos were far less regulated and some took advantage of that, slot techs had all kinds of tricks to prevent the big jackpot from being hit. For example, they used to spot weld the reel tabs so the mechanical fingers couldn't slide into the reel that completed the big-jackpot combination. Then there was the Gaming tech who fixed a machine to pay when a certain sequence of buttons was pushed.

Debbie Tosun Kilday

Even then, though, it wasn't so much the casinos that tried to gaff the machines not to pay off as it was the slot thieves who tried to gaff the machines to pay. One gang opened the machines and replaced the EPROMS right under the surveillance department's nose; the gang figured out that surveillance didn't have the right equipment to videotape that area of the casino.

Of course, as casinos are watched more closely, slots get more sophisticated, and surveillance gets more efficient, such incidents have become increasingly rare. But that doesn't mean it'll never happen again. Somewhere ... someone ... is working on a plan.

Question of the Day February 11, 2011

Q: Can you explain how a random number generator decides if any given spin on a slot machine is a winner or not? We keep reading about the "split second" timing you need to hit a jackpot, but what exactly does that mean?

A: Put on your thinking cap, because the answer to this question is technical, involving step motors, digital pulses, seed values, numerical remainders, and virtual reels. We ran it originally in 2006; here it is again.

The random number generator is a piece of software operated by a microprocessor in the computer in a slot or video poker machine. Think of your own computer, running a word-processing or spreadsheet program. Instead of these common functions, the slot machine's computer runs a program that cycles endlessly and speedily through billions of numbers.

Now, these numbers aren't truly random. They're more accurately known as "pseudo-random" numbers, because they're generated by an algorithm (a mathematical formula) that follows a specific pattern. The pattern produces numbers that *appear* to be random, since they have to pass several built-in tests for randomness.

For example, a good algorithm might generate numbers that don't repeat, have an adequate numeric distribution, and can't be predicted, unless you know both the formula and the initial, or seed, value. But for all practical purposes, the RNGs in gambling machines approximate randomness closely enough to fulfill their intended purpose. (Note that random-number generators are getting better, as seed numbers as well are now often generated randomly -- perhaps in conjunction with electrical noise or, on a computer, by averaging mouse movements.)

When it's running, the RNG is generating whole numbers from one digit to 10 or 11 digits (in the billions, in other words). It spits out numbers hundreds of times a second for a slot machine and shuffles the deck of cards hundreds of times a second for a video poker machine. At the very moment when you pull the handle or press the "spin" or "deal" button, the computer identifies the next numbers or card sequence in the RNG's cycle. On a three-reel slot, the three numbers identified by the computer correspond to the three reels of the slot machine. On a video poker machine, the number identifies the exact order of the playing cards, from first to last, in the deck.

Debbie Tosun Kilday

To further complicate matters, according to the website http://money.howstuffworks.com/slot-machine3.htm, it's not the number *itself* that corresponds to the reels or the deck. Rather the RNGs that operate slot machines go through a second step of simple (for a computer) arithmetic, feeding the numbers through another process to determine where the reels should stop. In the example provided by howstuffworks.com, the RNG number is divided by a set value, usually 32, 64, 128, 256, or 512, with the divisor corresponding to the number of virtual stops on the reel.

Say the RNG number is 12,345,678 and the computer divides by 128. It comes up with 96,450, with a remainder of 9. The *remainder* is the critical number: 9 now becomes the stop on the first virtual reel on the slot machine. The same exercise determines the stops for the second and third virtual reels.

Here's an extremely simplistic example of a virtual reel. The physical reel might have two different symbols, a blank that pays nothing and a bar that pays a jackpot. The virtual reel, meanwhile, has 128 stops, with 127 programmed to land on the blank and only one programmed to land on the bar.

Once the computer knows the remainders of the three numbers taken from the RNG's cycle, it then consults a table that tells it how far to move the physical reel to correspond with the stop on the virtual reel. This is where the step motor comes in. A short pulse of electricity moves the motor a precise increment to land the reel on the exact spot determined by the computer.

Thus, when you press the spin or deal button on a slot or video poker machine, you're initiating a speed-of-light sequence that instructs the computer to show the reel positions or card values that correspond to the last set of numbers generated by the RNG. The spinning reels on a slot machine and the cards of a video poker machine are, in the final analysis, for display purposes only. The true action is with the computer that determines the display.

Question of the Day May 6, 2011

Q: I watched a television show on cable about Las Vegas and gambling. Anthony Curtis was on it and someone was talking about players, sometimes called "customers" or "clients," that pay others to play for them (blackjack, video poker, craps, roulette, etc.). Over the years I've learned to play perfect video poker and would like to get in on this. Can you give me more information about this?

A: We've never heard the term "client," but it's obvious that the discussion was about playing with "backers." A backer (or "investor") is someone who finances a skilled player for a cut of the winnings. Backers will get involved in any game or gambling situation where skilled players have a mathematical expectation of coming out ahead over time. A player has to be known to be good enough to be backed, but when he is, it's a good way to build his own gambling stake, since the backer typically absorbs all losses if a profit isn't realized.

Debbie Tosun Kilday

Backers run the gamut from former players who've moved on to other things and want to continue earning from their field of expertise, to players who simply don't possess the skills to win, but have a lot of money and see this as a legitimate form of investing. It's very common in poker, where new players who exhibit skill seek to be "staked," either by other established poker players or by one of the big online poker sites. It's very common in poker tournaments, and in the late stages of a big events you'll hear people talking about how many "horses" they have left, meaning players they're staking that are in position to earn them money.

Using your video poker example, here's how it works. Your backer might give you $10,000 to play an opportunity where a progressive meter has gone positive. That $10,000 is called the "bank" and it might, depending on the deal, also be used to pay expenses like food or travel if the game is in another city.

Once the play is over (say the jackpot gets hit), the bank is "broken." If someone else hit the progressive, then you probably lost money and whatever remains is returned to the backer at that point. However, a "make-up" is usually in effect. That means that if you make a similar deal in the future and it's successful, the player doesn't get a share of the win until the prior loss is recouped.

If it's you that hits the progressive and there's a profit, it's shared according to the negotiated terms. The split percentages are structured in many different ways depending on the amount of the investment, time spent by the player, etc. (and it can get especially complicated in video poker because of the tax ramifications for

228

hitting big jackpots), but it's often as simple as cutting up the winnings 50/50.

Of course, trust is a paramount component in this type of arrangement. Since the backer is rarely in a position to monitor results, he's subject to false reporting and many a player-backer deal has dissolved over pure suspicion (there's an interesting story about this in Bob Dancer's Million Dollar Video Poker). Because of this, it's difficult to get someone to back you that you don't already know well.

Question of the Day July 22, 2011

Q: I have been told there is a patron saint of gamblers. Is there?

A: We were tempted to go with the answer submitted by a reader who saw today's QoD previewed and assumed the Patron Saint of Gamblers was Bob Dancer, but we thought better of it.

In fact, the recognized Patron Saint of Gamblers is Saint Cayetano or Cajetan, whose Feast Day is coming up on August 7. St Cayetano was born to well-to-do parents in Vicenza, Italy in 1480 and was inclined a life of piety by his mother. He studied law and worked as a diplomat for Pope Julius II, with whom he helped reconcile the Venetian Republic. He was ordained as a priest in 1516. We couldn't find much pertinent information about his life and why he was selected as the Patron Saint of Gamblers (not to mention the unemployed, job seekers, and good fortune), although

Debbie Tosun Kilday

one source explained that it was because people would bet him a rosary or blessed candle that he would not do some special favor for them. In his life Saint Cayetano gave his family fortune to help those in need and he promoted the spiritual life in conjunction with care for the poor and sick. According to Wikipedia, "he died of grief in Naples" in 1547, worn out by the corruption he saw around him, particularly within the priesthood. He was beatified in 1629 and canonized in 1671.

In the course of this research, we also came across San Simon, Guatemala's own Patron Saint of Gamblers and Drunks. Part Catholic saint and part Mayan god, his worshippers apparently pray to him for fertility and prosperity and his shrine, located in the village of San Andres Itzapa, apparently receives copious offerings of alcohol and tobacco (cash is also welcomed) from his devotees to appease him. A statue of him at the shrine is described as being covered in plastic because people "sometimes spit alcohol and Coca-Cola on him as a way to ask for his blessings." Nice.

Lastly, Saint Bernadine (or Bernadino) of Siena is known as the Patron Saint of Gambling Addicts and Compulsive Gambling, among many other things. A charismatic orator born in Massa di Carrara, Italy in 380, Saint Bernadine was known for his mediating abilities and skill at reconciling opponents, and for his numerous female supporters.

D.T.K. - My Tips on Playing
Slot Machines To Win

(I make no promises that you will win if you play as I suggest. The only thing I can say is it works for me most of the time.)

You plan on winning before you walk into the casino. The first step is to envision what you desire. If you plan on winning say so. Tell others you are going there to win.

While entering any casino I always would hear other people saying things like, "I am coming to make my weekly deposit to the casino" or "I never win anything."

Stop the negativity! Words are heard and the feelings they inspire are spread throughout the universe. Negativity creates an atmosphere for failure. If you go in as a loser you are not aspiring to be anything else but a loser.

Never go in thinking you are not capable or not lucky enough to win. Don't be afraid to 'be able'. Let go of the idea that you are not good enough.

Don't walk in and immediately sit down at just any machine and start playing. Be selective by first browsing the different areas of the casino. Try to see what types of machines are winning, even if they are winning small amounts. See what areas people congregate at.

Debbie Tosun Kilday

Whatever denomination machine, always play the maximum number of coins the machine takes. The machines win more consistently playing this way then when you play one coin. The machines recognize what amount of money you are playing for each spin and will win or lose accordingly. Some machines will come up with the huge jackpot when you play the minimum number of coins. That is to show you that you would have won but didn't because you did not play the maximum number of coins. Learn from others mistakes. I once played two coins in a three coin machine. I could have won ten thousand dollars if I had played three coins but I didn't because I had only played two coins. Don't let yourself have to see the huge jackpot come up on the face of the machine knowing that you can't claim it. Also know that when you do not play the max amount of coins that the machine allows, you are changing the programming so that it will take much longer before the machine hits the big jackpot. The machine will have to adjust for each less coin per spin and depending on how many times people played that way it will take that much longer to win.

If you must play penny machines (Which I try not to) at least try to play one with a progressive jackpot that is so large (2 million +) that you might have a chance at winning something significant. When progressive penny machines near the progressive jackpot amount they tend to win much larger amounts then they normally would.

The fact is penny machines win the least amount of money overall than any other type of machine in the casino. This is why all the casinos have loaded up on penny machines. I must mention that you **might** be

232

able to play a penny machine much longer with a small budget. No guarantees of that though. Some of the penny machines I have seen might cost you six dollars or more per spin.

Playing a hundred dollar machine you will most likely win more than five thousand dollars plus if in fact you win anything at all. It all depends on where the machine is at in its programming. It also depends on how many hundred dollar bills you have to spend waiting for a jackpot. The average person should never play hundred dollar machines.

I personally try to stick with playing dollar machines. If I am low on money I will play a quarter machine. If I end up making a lot of money playing the dollar machines I will then try my luck at the five dollar machines if I am feeling lucky. If you are not feeling the vibe, go home with your winnings and see what happens at your next visit.

If you don't have a big budget in which to play with, my advice is to play quarter machines rather than penny machines. Most quarter machines take anywhere from two to five coins for each spin. That means that the most you will have to play for each spin would be $1.25 a spin. The casinos pretty much leave quarter machines alone when adjusting and doing maintenance. You have a pretty good chance of winning anywhere from $500 to $1,000 playing a quarter machine. Remember that it all depends on how many coins and how many dollars went into the machine before you sat down to play.

When playing the different slot machines I try to adhere to certain rules that seem to work for me. Each machine knows what type of bill is put into the machine before you start playing. Depending on where the machine is in its programming it may be counting how many bills go in before it pays out the jackpot. For instance, it may wait to count ten bills going into the machine before it pays out a win. If you were to put a hundred dollar bill into a penny machine you might spend close to the hundred dollars before winning five dollars. That is not something that would be worthwhile.

I may in fact be superstitious. I hate to admit this but I never use fifty dollar bills at a casino. I have heard they are considered bad luck. I don't want to play with them and never have. I have observed other people playing with fifty dollar bills. In my experience I have not seen any of them win any jackpots at all.

Penny machines – Don't use anything more than a ten dollar bill.

Quarter machines – Don't use anything more than a twenty dollar bill.

Dollar machines and up – Use only hundred dollar bills.

When playing any machine it is a good sign if you are getting cherries. You must get several cherries within a short time span before the machine will pay out a bigger amount. It works this way each and every time.

To try to determine if a machine is near winning a significant amount try to notice if the reels are spinning fast or on the slow side. The difference is very slight but there is a difference. As the reels spin faster try to spin as fast and as often as you can. This will mean you will be winning a larger amount very soon.

When trying to decide which machine to sit down at and play try to sit at one that shows as many symbols or numbers as possible on the face of the machine. They don't have to be on the line. The numbers or symbols could be anywhere on the face of the machine. These machines have a shorter time frame before winning. If you see a symbol or number on the line on the far right position you have a better chance at winning playing that machine.

When playing a Blazing Seven machine there may be several times that the machine must play through a certain programming sequence. Look for several things to determine if it is playing the winning sets to possibly hit the progressive jackpot soon.

1. You must see three bars/lines in each position across on the line which is usually sixty dollars.
Note: On a quarter machine you would get one bar in each position across the line.
2. Look for three solid red sevens which would be three hundred dollars.
3. You will get several two dollar wins where two blazing sevens come up on the screen anywhere in the first and second positions starting from left to right. This is the same as getting a cherry if you were playing another type of machine.
4. Look for the crisscross.
From left to right - a blazing seven in the far upper left, blazing seven on the line in the middle position, blazing seven in the far lower right hand corner.
5. Several spins where you get nothing.
6. From left to right – a blazing seven in the lower left hand corner, a blazing seven on the line in the

middle position, a blazing seven in the upper right hand corner of the machine.

7. If the machine is ready to hit the progressive jackpot it will. If it has several more times where it has to go through the same sequence I hope you recognize that fact in time. If you don't recognize that fact you will be playing in the amount of the progressive jackpot before you again see numbers 1-5 above.

The thing to remember when playing these machines is to know that if you have just gotten three mixed sevens several times which would be a $200 win and three solid red sevens which is a $300 win.

You now have to ask yourself this question. "I just won almost the amount of the progressive jackpot, should I keep playing for fear I might lose it all before winning anything again?"

The smart thing to do is to cash out and try your luck on another blazing sevens machine or a different type of machine altogether. If you want to try to win the progressive jackpot and will only be satisfied after doing so, then don't listen to my advice.

Another tip concerning the Blazing Sevens that several of my friends say works is every time you win $200 or $300 dollars they cash out and start using a new hundred dollar bill. They believe this resets the machine and you will win more $200 and $300 wins. I don't usually use this tactic myself but at times I have seen that it works well for others, giving them several hundreds of dollars before they cash out.

One more thing about Blazing Sevens – the progressive jackpot amount goes up by one penny each time the slot machine spins. On a dollar Blazing Sevens machine the progressive jackpot amount usually does not exceed $1,300. I say **usually** because there was once a Blazing Sevens machine that I started playing at Foxwoods Casino thinking the progressive jackpot would happen shortly. The jackpot amount was at $1,340. That was very unusual but when I finally won the progressive jackpot it hit at $2,416. I attribute that happening to the fact that someone before me was only playing one or two coins in instead of the three coins it takes to win the progressive jackpot. Playing less than three coins prohibited the machine from winning the progressive amount by resetting the machine by one coin each and every time it was played that way.

Take my advice when I tell you to play the max coins in each and every time you play. You will be happy you did.

It is a good idea to get a Players Club Card before going off to play a slot machine.

Most people play a slot machine with their Players Club Card inserted each and every time they play. This is good for you and good for the casino. It is good for you because the longer you play the more points you will accumulate. The more points you accumulate, the more free casino perks you will be offered. Casinos allow you to use your accumulated points to purchase things like concert tickets, pay for your meals in their restaurants, buy clothing and other goods at the stores within the casino, etc. The casinos track your play each time your card goes into a slot machine anywhere in the casino.

The way it benefits the casino is they can reward you by offering you free perks after examining how much time and money you spent playing the slot machines.

They can upgrade your status and bring you to a higher level so that you receive better perks and even expensive free gifts. It also shows and keeps track of how many people are playing slot machines in their casino by tracking the Players Club Cards thus showing the overall health of the casino plus being able to reward their players that spend the most time there. For the most part it is a win, win situation for both you and the casino. I sometimes would remove my Players Club Card while playing certain slot machines, then insert it after spinning the machine one or two times. This would cause an interrupt or temporary glitch in the machine which would sometimes cause the machine to reset it's programming as it does when a new player starts playing the machine. At times this would cause the machine to pay out a jackpot sooner. This is only my personal opinion as to how these things work and how they affect playing and winning.

It all comes down to how much passion you have in what you do, how much love you have for the game, and how observant you want to be as to how successful you will become. In my observations most people do not want to do much thinking when arriving at a casino. They go to the casino for the fun activities it provides them. They meet up with friends, go to dinner and a show and at the end of the night, they may play a few slot machines or a table game.

Whatever your reasons might be for frequenting a casino I sincerely wish each and everyone, "Good Luck and Much Prosperity." As Spock would say, "Live long and prosper."

1. The W2G Slips From My Five Years of Taxable Wins

2. My Concert Ticket Stubs I Kept As Souvenirs

3. A Sampling Of My Concert Photos & Events At Casinos

End Notes

i. My first visit to Mohegan Sun and my first win of $10,000. while playing a dollar machine.

ii. This is a photo of the two bundles of money each containing $5,000 representing my first win of $10,000.

iii. The first time I played a five dollar machine and won a jackpot of $13,500.

iv. I entered a drawing at Mohegan Sun and my ticket was pulled out of a barrel. I won the first prize of $20,000.

v. I convinced Mike to keep playing this dollar machine and he was glad he did after winning the $10,000 jackpot.

vi. A photo of me winning yet another $1,000 jackpot on a dollar machine.

Debbie Tosun Kilday

vii. Another win of a $10,000 jackpot, playing a Bonus Times machine at Mohegan Sun.

viii. A photo of Mike and I in Las Vegas at the Las Vegas Hilton with me winning another $10,000 jackpot.

ix. A Photo I took of Mike at Hoover Dam while visiting Las Vegas, rubbing the feet of the 'Angels of the Dam' statues for good luck.

x. After getting off the plane returning from Las Vegas, I went to Mohegan Sun before heading home only to win yet another $10,000 jackpot.

Made in the USA
Charleston, SC
12 September 2013